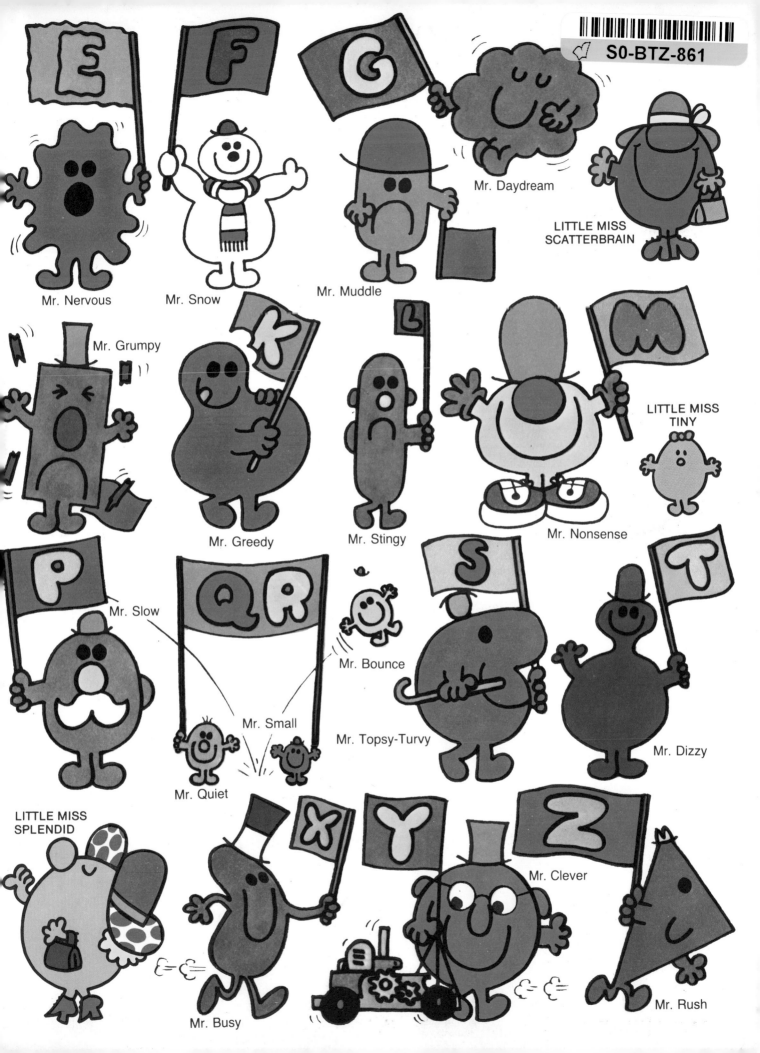

# MR. MEN™
# AND LITTLE MISS™
# PICTURE
# DICTIONARY

# MR. MEN™ AND LITTLE MISS™ PICTURE DICTIONARY

Roger Hargreaves

**PRICE/STERN/SLOAN**
Publishers, Inc., Los Angeles
1984

# INTRODUCTION

Thousands of children have been captivated and entertained by the famous Mr. Men™ and Little Miss™ books. The characters created by Roger Hargreaves are instantly appealing and their popularity remains with each child for a considerable time. The books are returned to again and again, which confirms that the stories provide a most satisfying experience for children. The fun, the laughter, the mistakes and escapes, so dominant in all the books, have encouraged many children to read and enjoy reading.

This new and exciting MR. MEN™ AND LITTLE MISS™ PICTURE DICTIONARY has been compiled to encourage children in developing further reading skills. All the familiar characters appear throughout its pages, in lively illustrations that will stimulate and maintain interest in the dictionary. Very young children will discover that they can learn to 'read' the words because the pictures present accurate clues. For older children, the dictionary will provide endless opportunities to learn how to spell words they wish to write and to find out the meanings of unfamiliar words. Finally, by constantly using this delightful dictionary, children will quickly appreciate a sense of alphabetical order, which is a very important skill to master.

The MR. MEN™ AND LITTLE MISS™ PICTURE DICTIONARY is both simple and attractive, which ensures that children will enjoy using it and will learn so much from it.

## a

A means any one thing. This book is a dictionary.

## able

To be able to do something means that you can do it. It is important to be able to read.

## about

About means having something to do with. This book is about words.

About also means nearly. Mr. Happy thought it was about three o'clock. His watch showed it was five minutes to three.

## above

Above means over or higher than. There is a picture of Mr. Slow above Mr. Lazy's bed.

above

## absent

Absent means away or not here. If you are ill, you may be absent from school.

## absent-minded

Absent-minded means forgetful. Little Miss Scatterbrain is absent-minded.

## absolutely

Absolutely means completely. Mr. Clumsy was absolutely soaked when he slipped and fell into the swimming pool.

## absurd

Absurd means silly or ridiculous.

## accept

To accept something is to receive it or agree to it. Mr. Happy accepted Mr. Greedy's invitation and went to his party.

## accident

An accident is something that is not expected to happen. Mr. Bump is always having accidents. He broke the kitchen window, but he did not mean to.

## ache

An ache is a pain. You may get a stomach ache if you eat too many apples.

## across

Across means from one side to the other. Mr. Topsy-Turvy walked backwards across the street.

across

## act

To act is to do something or to do something in a special way. Mr. Silly always acts foolish. His actions are ridiculous.

Acting also means playing a part. An actor or actress is a person who pretends to be someone in a film or play.

An act is a section of a play.

An act is also a law, like an act of Congress.

## active

Active means doing a lot. Mr. Busy is active from morning until night. He is always busy with one activity or another.

## add

To add is to put one or more things with other things. You add sugar to tea to make it taste sweet. Adding numbers together is called addition. Mr. Clever added two and two and made four.

## address

Your address is made up of the number of your house, the name of the street and the city and state in which you live. When you send a letter you need to put the correct address on the envelope.

address

Mr. Sneeze
Frosty Cottage
1 High Street
Shivertown

## admire

To admire something is to think it is very good. Mr. Happy admired Mr. Uppity's car. He thought it was the nicest car he had ever seen.

## admit

To admit to something is to say that you have done it. Mr. Clumsy admitted that he had broken two of Mr. Fussy's plates. He was very sorry.

To admit also means to let in. Dogs are not usually admitted to food stores.

## adopt

To adopt means to take as your own. Sometimes people adopt other people's children and look after them as part of their own family.

## adore

To adore means to love very much.

## adult

An adult is a person who has grown up. Another name for an adult is a grown-up.

## advantage

An advantage is something that is useful or helpful to you. It is an advantage to be given a head start in a race.

## adventure

An adventure is an exciting or dangerous experience. Mr. Daydream told about an adventure in Africa. He was nearly eaten by a crocodile, but he got away.

## advertise

To advertise something is to make it known to people. You can advertise something you want to sell or an event you want people to attend.

## advise

To advise is to suggest what to do. The doctor advised Mr. Bounce to wear heavy shoes to keep him from bouncing all over the place. That was good advice!

Mr. Small has an advantage in this race. He is starting in front of all the other runners.

## afford

To afford is to have enough money to buy something. Mr. Stingy said he couldn't afford to buy any furniture. But he had a boxful of money hidden away, so he really could have afforded some.

## afraid

Afraid means frightened. Mr. Worry is always afraid something terrible will happen.

## after

After means later than. Mr. Strong feels stronger than ever after he has eaten a plateful of eggs.

## afternoon

The afternoon is the part of the day between noon and evening.

## afterwards

Afterwards means at a later time. A giant made Mr. Greedy eat the most enormous meal he had ever seen. Mr. Greedy felt very ill afterwards.

## again

Again means once more. Mr. Messy looked quite clean after he had a bath. But he soon got dirty again.

## against

Against means touching. Mr. Clumsy leaned against a door that had just been painted. He got paint all over his arm.

Against also means opposite to. Our football team plays against another team every week.

## age

The age of something is how old it is. Many children start school at the age of five.

## ago

Ago means past or before now. Two hundred years ago there were no cars and no airplanes. The train left the station a minute ago.

## agree

To agree with someone is to think the same way. The people of Tiddletown all agreed that Mr. Nosey was far too nosey for his own good.

against

## ahead

Ahead means in front. When you are winning a race, you are ahead of all the others.

## aim

To aim is to point towards something you are trying to hit. Mr. Clever is aiming an arrow at the target.

## air

Air is what you take into your lungs when you breathe. It is all around but usually you cannot feel it or see it. You open a window to let fresh air into a room.

airplane

## airplane

An airplane is a machine that flies in the air and takes people and packages to and from faraway places.

aim

## alarm

An alarm is a loud noise that warns people of danger.

An alarm clock makes a noise to wake you up. Mr. Noisy's alarm clock is so loud, it wakes up everyone in town!

## album

An album is a book you put things in that you want to keep, such as photographs or stamps.

## alike

Alike means the same. Little Miss Neat and Mr. Fussy are alike in that they are both clean and tidy.

alarm

## alive

Alive means living, not dead. Plants and animals need water to stay alive.

all

## all

All means everything. If Mr. Greedy eats all the candies in the jar he will make himself sick.

## allow

To allow means to let someone do something. I am allowed to watch television until bedtime.

## almost

Almost means nearly. Mr. Small can almost reach Mr. Bounce's doorbell, but he is not quite tall enough.

almost

## alone

Alone means on your own. Mr. Chatterbox doesn't like being alone. When he is alone, he has no one to talk to.

## along

Along means from one end to the other. There is a row of flowers growing along the edge of Mr. Fussy's lawn.

along

## aloud

Aloud means in a voice that can be heard. When you read a story aloud, other people can hear you.

## alphabet

The alphabet is the 26 letters from A to Z.

## already

Already means by this time. Little Miss Late went to help Mr. Busy paint his house. But Mr. Busy had already finished by the time she arrived.

## also

Also means as well. This book is about words. It is also about Mr. Men and Little Misses.

### although
Although means in spite of something. Although he couldn't swim, Mr. Tall went to the pool with Mr. Small.

### altogether
Altogether means when everyone or everything is counted.

### always
Always means all the time. Mr. Worry always has a problem and never stops worrying.

### amaze
To amaze is to surprise someone very much. Mr. Nonsense was amazed to see Mr. Impossible walking on the ceiling.

### ambulance
An ambulance is a type of car used to take people who have been hurt or are ill to the hospital.

### among
Among means in the middle of a group. Mr. Quiet's house is among the trees.

### amount
An amount is the total of a number of things.

The wizard is taking a photograph of the Mr. Men and Little Misses altogether.

13

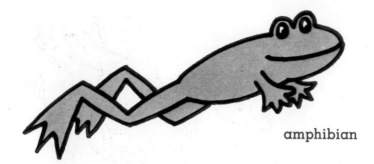

amphibian

## amphibian
An amphibian is a cold-blooded animal that spends part of its life on land and part in the water. Frogs are amphibians.

## amuse
To amuse is to please someone or to keep someone busy in a pleasant way. Mr. Funny amused Mr. Silly by making faces.

## an
An means one. It takes all day for Mr. Slow to eat an apple.

## and
And means also. There are short words and long words in this dictionary.

amuse

## angry
Angry means very upset. Mr. Fussy was angry with Mr. Mischief for digging a hole in the lawn.

## animal
An animal is any living creature that moves about. Birds, fish, insects, reptiles, and mammals are all animals.

ankle

## ankle
Your ankle is the part of your body between your foot and leg.

## announce
To announce is to tell something to people. The principal announced that school was going to close early.

## annoy
To annoy is to make someone cross. Mr. Busy was annoyed because Mr. Lazy was so slow.

## another
Another means one more. Mr. Greedy is wondering whether he can find room for another cake. He has eaten four already!

## answer
An answer is a reply to a question. Mr. Happy asked Mr. Topsy-Turvy how he was feeling. Mr. Topsy-Turvy answered, "You thank, very well."

## ant
An ant is a small insect.

## any
Any means some. Mr. Skinny didn't eat any breakfast. He didn't eat anything all day.

## anxious
Anxious means worried. Mr. Worry was anxious when it rained because he thought his roof might leak.

apart

## apart
Apart means away from each other. Mr. Silly and Mr. Nonsense do not live very far apart.

Apart also means into pieces. Mr. Clumsy did not mean to break the chair. It just came apart in his hands!

## apologize
To apologize is to say you are sorry. Mr. Grumpy did not apologize to Mr. Happy for stepping on his toe. He wasn't sorry at all. He did it on purpose!

## appear
To appear means to come into sight.

To appear also means to seem to be. Mr. Grumpy always appears bad-tempered. Mr. Happy has a happy appearance.

## appetite
An appetite is a feeling of wanting to eat. Little Miss Plump has a very big appetite. She is always hungry.

## applaud
To applaud is to clap your hands to show that you like something. People applaud at the end of a concert or play.

## apple
apple

An apple is a round fruit that grows on trees. Most apples are good to eat.

## approach
To approach something is to go near it.

## approve
To approve of something is to be pleased with it. Mr. Greedy approved of Mr. Happy's idea to have a picnic in the park.

## apron
An apron is a piece of cloth worn over clothes to keep them clean.

## aquarium
An aquarium is a container of water used for keeping fish.

## area
An area is an amount of space. A school playground is usually a large area.

arm

### argue

To argue is to say that you do not agree with someone. Mr. Silly and Mr. Nonsense had an argument about what to have for dinner. Mr. Nonsense wanted cornflake pie and Mr. Silly wanted apple stew.

### arithmetic

Arithmetic is working with numbers.

### arm

Your arm is the part of your body between your shoulder and hand. Mr. Tickle has extremely long arms.

### army

An army is a large number of soldiers who fight together against an enemy.

### around

Around means on all sides. Mr. Bump has bandages around his head and body.

### arrange

To arrange is to put something in order. In this dictionary the words are arranged in alphabetical order.

To arrange also means to plan. Mr. Busy made arrangements to meet Mr. Slow at six o'clock, but Mr. Slow was late as usual.

### arrest

To arrest is to take someone to the police station because he or she has done something wrong.

### arrive

To arrive is to reach somewhere. Mr. Rush ran all the way to the station to catch his train. He arrived two hours early!

### arrow

An arrow is a straight stick with a point at one end and feathers at the other. It is shot from a bow.

An arrow is also a sign that points the way to go.

arrest

## art

Art is drawing and painting.

Art is the ability to do something very well.

An artist is a person who makes beautiful things or performs extremely well.

## article

An article is a thing or a piece of something. A dress is an article of clothing.

An article is also a story that appears in a magazine or a newspaper.

## artificial

Artificial means made by people not by nature. Real flowers grow and die. Artificial flowers are made of plastic, paper or other materials.

## ashamed

Ashamed means feeling upset and sorry because you have done something wrong.

The children assembled to hear the principal's good news.

## ask

To ask is to put a question to somebody. Mr. Happy asked Mr. Grumpy if he knew how to smile.

## asleep

Asleep means sleeping and not awake. Mr. Lazy spends most of the day asleep.

## assemble

To assemble is to put or to come together. The children assembled in the auditorium before lunch to hear the principal speak.

## assist

To assist is to help someone. A nurse is often a doctor's assistant.

## astronaut

An astronaut is someone who travels in space.

## at

At tells where something or someone is. There was a box at Little Miss Splendid's door.

At also tells the time of something. We will eat at 6 o'clock.

## attack

To attack means to start fighting. Mr. Nervous thought he was being attacked by a man-eating snake, but it was only a friendly worm!

## attend

To attend is to be present. The teacher knows who attends school every day. He or she keeps a record of attendance.

To attend is also to take care of.

## attention

Attention is giving care. To pay attention is to listen and watch carefully. You pay attention to what the teacher says in school.

## attic

An attic is a room or space just under the roof of a house.

## attract

To attract means to draw to something. Mr. Noisy attracts attention with his loud voice.

autumn

## audience

An audience is the people who listen to music or watch a play, movie or circus.

## aunt

Your aunt is the sister of your mother or your father, or your uncle's wife.

## automobile

An automobile is a car.

## autumn

Autumn is the season of the year that comes between summer and winter.

## avenue

An avenue is a street.

## avoid

To avoid is to keep away from. When Mr. Bump stepped sideways to avoid a puddle, he slipped and fell in the mud.

## awake

Awake means not asleep. Mr. Lazy is nearly always asleep. He is not awake very often.

## away

Away means not there. Mr. Nonsense went to Mr. Silly's house, but Mr. Silly was away.

Away also means far from. Mr. Silly was at the beach, forty miles away.

## awful

Awful means very bad. Mr. Messy's house is in an awful mess.

## ax

An ax is a tool used for chopping wood. It has a handle at one end and a sharp metal blade at the other end.

ax

## baby
A baby is a very young child. Babies need special care.

## back
The back of something is the part furthest away from the front. Mr. Slow is at the back of the line.

back

Your back is the part of your body that is behind you.

Back also means return. You take a book back to the library after you have read it.

## backwards
If someone is moving backwards, he is moving with his back first. Mr. Topsy-Turvy sometimes walks backwards.

## bad
Bad means not good. Mr. Mischief has the bad habit of playing tricks on everyone.

## bag
A bag is used for carrying things. A shopping bag has handles and holds many packages.

## bake
To bake is to cook food in a hot oven. A baker bakes bread and cakes for people to buy at his or her bakery.

## balance
To balance is to stay steady and not fall over. To ride a bicycle you have to keep your balance.

## bald
Bald means having no hair on the top of the head.

Mr. Noisy is leading the Wobbletown band.
He loves the loud, noisy music.

## ball

A ball is a round object to play with. Balls are used in games like football, tennis and golf.

A ball is also a party with dancing.

## balloon

A balloon is a rubber-like bag that stretches when you blow air into it.

## banana

A banana is a fruit that grows in bunches on trees in hot countries. Bananas are long and soft and have thick yellow skins.

## band

A band is a group of people who play musical instruments together.

A band is also a strip of material used to hold things together, like a rubber band.

## bandage

A bandage is a strip of clean white material. You put bandages around bad cuts to keep them clean. Mr. Bump is always covered in bandages.

## bang

A bang is a sudden noise made by bumping or hitting something.

## bank

A bank is a piece of sloping ground. There are banks on both sides of a river.

Another kind of bank is a place where people put their money to save it and to keep it safe.

## bar

A bar is a solid piece of something, like a bar of soap.

A bar is also a counter or a store where food and drinks are served.

To bar means to stop someone or something from passing through or doing something.

### bare
Something that is bare has nothing on it.

### bark
To bark is to make the noise that a dog makes.

Bark is also the rough covering on the trunk and branches of a tree.

### barn
A barn is a building on a farm. Farmers put hay in barns to keep it dry.

### baseball
Baseball is a popular team game played with a bat and a ball.

bat

### bat
A bat is a wooden object with a handle used to hit a ball in games, like baseball.

Another kind of bat is a small furry mammal that flies at night.

### bath
A bath is a big tub that you fill with water and sit in. When you have a bath, you wash yourself all over. Mr. Messy has to take a bath every day.

### battered
Battered means knocked around and damaged. Mr. Clumsy's suitcase is battered because he has dropped it so many times.

### battle
A battle is a fight between people or armies.

### be
To be is to live or to exist. To be is also to act or to feel. There are many forms of **be**. Can you **be** happy? I **am** happy today. Mr. Happy **is** always happy. Many of his friends **are** happy, too. **Being** happy is a very good feeling. Mr. Happy **has been** happy for a long time. It **was** very hard for Mr. Grumpy to **be** happy about anything.

barn

### basin
A basin is a deep bowl. Basins are used for washing things in.

### basket
A basket is used to carry or hold things. Baskets are made of pieces of bent wood or straw woven together.

beach

## beach
A beach is the strip of sand at the edge of an ocean or a lake. Mr. Happy went to the beach with his friends.

## beads
Beads are small round balls or fancy shaped bits which you string together to make jewelry.

## beak
A beak is a bird's mouth. Beaks are hard.

## bean
A bean is a vegetable. Beans are the seeds and sometimes the seed pods of plants like string beans and coffee beans.

## bear
A bear is a large furry mammal. Young bears are called cubs.

If you can't bear something, it means you don't like it. Mr. Slow can't bear to be rushed.

To bear also means to hold something up or to carry it. If you climb a tree, you must make sure that the branches can bear your weight.

## beard
A beard is the hair that grows on a man's chin and cheeks.

## beat
To beat someone is to win. Mr. Rush beat Mr. Slow in a race. Mr. Slow gets beaten every time.

To beat also means to hit something over and over again. On a stormy day, the waves beat against the shore.

## beautiful
Beautiful means lovely to look at. On a clear day there is a beautiful view from the top of the hill.

## because
Because means for the reason that. Mr. Small had to leave his job at the candy store because he fell into the jars.

## bed
A bed is a piece of furniture that you sleep on. It has a soft mattress and pillows to make you comfortable.

## bee
A bee is an insect that makes a buzzing noise. Bees make honey and can sting if they are annoyed.

## beef
Beef is meat from a cow or bull.

## beet
A beet is a root vegetable that is a deep red color.

This dog is begging for a biscuit.

bee

## beetle
A beetle is an insect with four wings. The front wings form a hard case that protects the folded back wings.

## before
Before means earlier than. Mr. Forgetful forgot to put a stamp on his letter before he mailed it.

## beg
To beg is to ask for something you want very much. When a dog begs, he sits up on his back legs and raises his front paws.

## begin
To begin means to start. Mr. Lazy was just beginning to mow his lawn when it began to rain. He went back to bed instead!

## behave
To behave well is to be good. To behave badly is to be naughty. Little Miss Naughty never behaves herself. Her behavior is not very good.

## behind
Behind means in back of. Mr. Nosey is hiding behind a tree.

## believe
To believe something is to be sure that it is true. Not many people believe that ghosts exist.

## bell
A bell is an object that makes a ringing sound. You ring the bell on a bus to tell the driver to stop.

behind

## belong
Something that belongs to you is owned by you. Your clothes belong to you. They are your belongings.

## below
Below means under or lower than. Pete Worm is in the ground below Mr. Small's house.

## belt
A belt is a strip of leather or other material that you wear around your waist.

## bend
To bend is not to be straight. You bend your knees when you kneel down.

Mr. Tall bent his knees to talk to Mr. Small.

## beside
Beside means next to. Mr. Chatterbox sat beside Mr. Quiet on the bus and chattered all the way to town.

## besides
Besides means also. When Mr. Greedy had breakfast, he ate a whole box of cornflakes besides three eggs and nine slices of toast!

## best
Best means of the highest quality. Kathy is the best reader in the class. She reads better than everyone else.

## better
Better means improved or in a more excellent way. Mr. Greedy was sick after his party, but he soon felt better.

below

## berry
A berry is a small fruit that grows on bushes. There are many kinds of berries.

between

24

## between

Between means in the middle. Mr. Clever is standing between Mr. Wrong and Mr. Grumpy.

## bicycle

A bicycle is a vehicle with two wheels and two pedals. You push the pedals with your feet to make the wheels go around.

## big

Big means large. An elephant is a big animal. A female elephant is bigger than its baby.

## bill

A bill is another name for a bird's beak.

A bill is also paper money, like a five dollar bill.

Another kind of bill shows how much money you have to pay for something. The carpenter fixed Mr. Happy's chair and sent him a bill for three dollars.

## bird

A bird is an animal that has feathers, two legs, and two wings. Most birds can fly. Sparrows, penguins, and chickens are all birds.

## birthday

Your birthday is the day you were born. Birthday cards and birthday presents are sent to people to celebrate this day each year.

## bit

A bit is a small piece. Mr. Fussy was annoyed to find a bit of mud on his carpet after he had just cleaned it.

bite

## bite

To bite something is to cut it with your teeth. Mr. Greedy has taken a large bite of his chocolate bar.

birthday

### black

Black is the darkest color. The words on this page are printed in black ink.

### blade

A blade is the sharp metal part of a knife.

A blade is also a leaf of grass.

### blame

To blame someone for something is to say it is his or her fault. When Mr. Happy's chair fell to pieces he blamed Mr. Mischief.

### blanket

A blanket is a soft warm cover for a bed. Mr. Sneeze has to have lots of blankets on his bed because he lives in Coldland.

blanket

### blaze

To blaze is to burn very brightly. A fire will blaze if you put dry twigs on it.

### bleed

To bleed is to lose blood. You usually bleed when you have a cut.

### blind

Blind means not able to see. Sometimes blind people have guide dogs to help them find their way.

A blind is a window covering used to keep the sun out.

### blink

To blink is to shut your eyes and open them again very quickly. A flash of bright light may make you blink.

### bliss

Bliss is feeling very happy.

### block

To block means to get in the way. Mr. Strong moved a fallen tree that was blocking the road.

A block is a big lump of something like stone or wood.

A block can also be the section of the street you live on.

block

## blood

Blood is red liquid that flows through your body.

## blossom

A blossom is a flower on a tree or a bush.

## blouse

A blouse is a kind of shirt that women and girls wear with skirts or trousers.

## blow

To blow is to push air out through the mouth or nose. When Mr. Strong went to blow out the candles on his birthday cake, he blew the cake right out of the window!

To blow is also to be carried by air. The snow was blown away by a strong wind.

A blow is a hard knock made with the fist.

A blow can be a shock or disappointment. It would be a blow to Mr. Greedy if the bakery went out of business!

blue

## blue

Blue is the color of the sky on a sunny day.

To be blue is also to be sad.

## blunt

Blunt means dull or not sharp. It is hard to draw a thin line with a blunt pencil.

Blunt also means frank and direct. People who speak bluntly may seem rude.

## blush

To blush is to go red in the face. People blush when they have done something silly, or when they feel embarrassed or shy.

## board

A board is a long flat piece of wood.

A board is also a piece of wood or heavy paper used for playing games like chess or checkers.

## boast

To boast is to talk a lot about yourself and all the things you can do.

## boat

A boat is used to travel on water. A row boat has oars to push it along. A sail boat has a sail to catch the wind which moves the boat along.

boat

## body

A body is all the parts of a person or an animal.

A body is also one whole thing. An ocean is a body of water.

## boil

To boil water is to heat it until it starts to bubble.

## bomb

A bomb is a hollow case filled with explosive material. A bomb explodes when it is dropped.

## bone

Bone is the hard part of the body of a person or animal that gives it its shape.

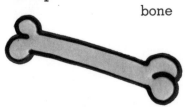

bone

## book

A book is made up of pages fastened between two covers. You read a story book. You write in a notebook.

## boomerang

A boomerang is a flat piece of wood that is bent in the middle. If you throw it in a special way it will come back to you.

## boot

A boot is a shoe that covers part of your leg as well as your foot.

## bore

To bore a hole is to make a hole with a sharp instrument.

To be bored means having nothing interesting to do. When Mr. Tickle is bored he goes looking for someone to tickle.

## born

To be born is to come into the world as a baby. Baby animals are quite weak when they have just been born.

## borrow

To borrow is to take something from someone to use and then give it back. Mr. Happy wanted to borrow Mr. Grumpy's lawn mower, but Mr. Grumpy wouldn't lend it to him.

## both

Both means the two together. You love both your mother and your father.

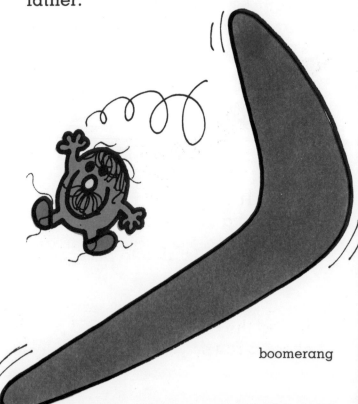

boomerang

## bottle

A bottle usually has a narrow top and is used to hold liquid. Bottles are made of glass or plastic.

## bottom

The bottom is the lowest or underneath part of something. Mr. Clumsy tripped over his shoelaces and fell all the way down the stairs to the bottom.

bottle

## bounce

To bounce means to spring back into the air after hitting something. Mr. Bounce is like a rubber ball. He bounces wherever he goes.

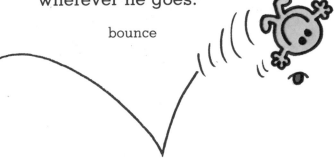
bounce

## bow (It rhymes with go.)

A bow is a knot with loops. Mr. Fussy ties his shoelaces in neat little bows.

A bow is also a piece of bent wood with a string tied from one end to the other and is used to shoot arrows.

## bow (It rhymes with now.)

To bow is to bend your body forward at the waist. People bow to the king or queen.

Bow also means the front end of a boat.

## bowl

A bowl is a round dish. Mr. Greedy ate a huge bowl of ice cream for dessert and was still hungry!

To bowl is to play a game by rolling a ball to knock down wooden sticks called pins. Bowling is a popular sport.

## box

A box is a container with sides and a bottom. A box usually has a lid.

To box is to fight someone. Both boxers wear special gloves called boxing gloves.

## brace

A brace is a strap that holds things together or straightens something like a tooth or a leg or an arm.

box

## bracelet

A bracelet is a band or chain worn around the wrist as jewelry.

## brain

The brain is the part of the body of a person or animal that is inside the head. It controls the actions of the body. People think, learn and remember with their brains.

## brake

A brake is used to slow or stop the movement of wheels on cars, trains, or bicycles. Most brakes work by pressing a pad against the wheel.

## branch

Branches are the parts of a tree that grow out from the trunk.

Mr. Silly is standing on a branch.

## brass

Brass is a yellow or gold mixture of the metals copper and zinc.

## brave

Brave means not afraid to do something difficult and dangerous.

## bread

Bread is a food made by mixing flour and water and then baking it in an oven. You can cut bread into slices to make sandwiches or toast.

## break

To break something is to make it come apart. Mr. Clumsy is always breaking things.

## breakfast

Breakfast is the first meal of the day. Mr. Skinny eats just one cornflake for breakfast.

This is Mr. Skinny's breakfast. One cornflake!

## breathe

To breathe is to take in air through your nose or mouth and let it out again. You breathe more quickly when you have been running because you are out of breath.

## breeze

A breeze is the wind blowing lightly.

brown

## brick

A brick is a heavy block of hard clay or stone. Bricks are used for building.

## bridge

A bridge is a pathway built across a river, a road, or a railway so that people can get from one side to the other safely and easily.

## brief

Brief means short, in time. Brief also means using few words.

## bright

Bright means filled with a lot of light. On a fine day the sun shines brightly in the sky.

Bright also means clever or smart. Mr. Clever thinks he is the brightest person in town.

## bring

To bring means to carry something with you. Mr. Stingy and Mr. Forgetful are having a picnic. Mr. Forgetful forgot to bring his food. Mr. Stingy only brought half a sandwich.

bring

## broom

A broom is a kind of brush with a long handle used to sweep the floor.

## brother

Your brother is a boy who has the same parents you do.

## brown

Brown is a color that is a mixture of red and green.

## bruise

A bruise is a dark mark on the skin, caused by bumping into something. Mr. Bump is covered with bruises.

## brush

A brush is a tool with stiff hairs at one end and a handle at the other. There are many kinds of brushes, like hairbrushes, toothbrushes, and paintbrushes.

## bubble

A bubble is a ball of liquid with air inside it.

## bucket

A bucket is a container with a handle used to carry water.

## build

To build is to make something by putting parts together. Mr. Clever built his own house.

bull

## bull

A bull is a large male mammal that has horns. Cows belong to the same family as bulls.

## bully

A bully is a person who is cruel to others, especially if they are smaller.

## bump

To bump into something is to knock into it by accident. Mr. Bump had a bruise on his head after he bumped into a door.

## bun

A bun is a sweet or plain bread.

## bunch

A bunch is a group of things held together.

Mr. Quiet is holding a bunch of flowers.

## bundle

A bundle is a package or a group of things tied or wrapped together.

## burglar

A burglar is a person who breaks into other people's houses and steals things.

## burn

To burn is to be on fire. Logs burn in a fireplace.

To burn is to give heat or to feel heat, like getting sunburned.

To burn also means to cook too long. Mr. Forgetful burned his bread because he forgot to take it out of the oven. The bread was burned.

## burst

To burst is to break open. Balloons burst if you put too much air into them or if you prick them with a pin.

## bury

To bury something is to put it into the ground and cover it up.

bus

## bus

A bus is a large car that has lots of seats. People pay to ride on buses.

## bush

A bush is a small tree with branches that grow close to the ground. Little Miss Neat trims her bushes very carefully.

## business

Business is the work people do to make a living.

A person's business is the private things that matter to him or her only. Mr. Nosey is always poking his nose into other people's business.

## busy

Busy means doing lots of things all the time. Mr. Busy has no time to sit and daydream. He is always busily cleaning the house, mowing the lawn, and washing the dishes.

## but

But means yet. Mr. Greedy always eats too much, but he never gets sick.

But also means except. Everyone was on time but Little Miss Late.

## butcher

A butcher is a person who cuts and sells meat.

## butter

Butter is a spread made from cream. You can put it on bread.

## butterfly

A butterfly is an insect with a thin body and four large wings.

butterfly

## button

A button is a small round object. Buttons are sewn on clothes to fasten them.

Buttons are also flat knobs that you press to make something work.

## buy

To buy is to get something by paying money for it. Mr. Greedy bought three cakes and six rolls.

## by

By means near or near to and past. Mr. Noisy and Mr. Chatterbox stood side by side. Mr. Busy rushed by them.

By also means how something was done or who did it. The cake was baked by putting it into a hot oven. It was baked by Mr. Greedy.

butcher

cabbage

## cabbage

A cabbage is a vegetable with green or purple leaves that form a round head.

## cabin

A cabin is a small house.

A cabin is also a small room on a ship, or the passenger part of an airplane.

## cabinet

A cabinet is a piece of furniture with shelves and drawers.

## cafe

A cafe is a restaurant where you can buy a snack or a drink.

## cage

A cage is a metal or wooden enclosure for keeping animals.

## cake

A cake is a sweet food made from flour and eggs and baked in an oven.

## calamity

A calamity is a great disaster. When Mr. Nervous hears the slightest noise, he thinks it is a calamity such as an earthquake.

## calendar

A calendar is a list or chart of the days and months of the year.

## calf

A young cow or bull is called a calf. Calves graze near their mothers.

A calf is also the back part of your leg, between the knee and the ankle.

calf

## call

To call means to speak in a loud voice. Mr. Dizzy called for help when a bull chased him.

To call also means to give something or someone a name. Mr. Men and Little Misses are all called different names.

To call on is to visit someone.

To call is also to telephone someone.

## camel

A camel is a large mammal that has one or two humps on its back.

## camera

A camera is used for taking photographs. It has a lens at the front and film inside.

Mr. Clever is taking a picture of Mr. Mischief with a camera.

## camp

A camp is a group of cabins, tents, or trailers where people live for a time.

To camp out is to live in the open air.

## can

If you can do something you are able to do it. Mr. Rush can clean his house in five minutes. Mr. Slow could never do that.

A can is a container usually made of metal, as in a can of beans.

## canal

A canal is a river-like body of water made by people. Boats travel along canals.

## candle

A candle is a stick of wax with a wick, or piece of string, running through the middle and sticking out at the top. The wick is lit and burns to give light.

## candy

Candy is a sweet, sugary food. Candies come in different sizes, shapes, and flavors.

## canoe

A canoe is a light, narrow boat you move through the water with a paddle.

## cap

A cap is a kind of hat. Policemen and nurses wear caps.

A cap is also a cover for a bottle.

## capital

A capital is a large letter. A B C are capital letters; a b c are small letters.

The capital of a country, or a state, is an important city.

## capsize

To capsize is to turn over accidentally. Boats capsize.

capsize

## captain

A captain is the person in charge. The captain of a team is the leader of the team.

## capture

To capture a person or animal is to catch and hold him or her prisoner.

## car

A car is a vehicle powered by an engine. An automobile is a car. Railroad cars are part of a train pulled by an engine.

car

## card

A card is a piece of stiff paper. You send greeting cards to wish people Happy Birthday and Merry Christmas.

When you go on a trip, you send postcards showing pictures of the places you have visited.

Playing cards are used for card games.

Cardboard is stiff paper used to make boxes.

## care

To care for means to like. I care for my baby brother very much.

To care for or to take care of means to look after. Sometimes I take care of my brother.

Care also means to want. Mr. Messy does not care to keep his house clean. Mr. Fussy takes good care of his house.

## careful

Careful means thinking about what you are doing so you don't make a mistake or have an accident. If Mr. Clumsy were more careful, he would not break so many things. Mr. Clumsy is careless.

## carol

Carols are the songs that are sung at Christmas.

## carpet

A carpet is a covering for the floor. Carpets are usually made of wool or nylon.

## carriage

A carriage is a baby's bed on wheels or a vehicle drawn by horses.

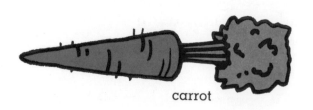

carrot

### carrot

A carrot is a long, thin, orange vegetable that grows in the ground. The part you eat is the root.

### carry

When you carry something, you hold it and take it from one place to another. Mr. Strong carried Mr. Muddle's suitcase for him because it was very heavy.

### cart

A cart is an open box with wheels that is pushed or pulled along.

carry

### cartoon

A cartoon is a story or a film told with drawings. Most cartoons make you laugh.

### carve

To carve is to cut carefully. You carve a turkey for dinner.

### case

A case is a box for things. You carry your clothes in a suitcase.

A case also refers to illness, such as a case of measles.

castle

### castle

A castle is a large building with strong, high walls. Castles were built many years ago for kings and queens and rich people.

### cat

Cats are mammals with thick fur and sharp claws. Young cats are called kittens.

### catch

To catch is to get hold of something. Mr. Clever can catch a ball with one hand. He has caught many balls that way.

caterpillar

### caterpillar

Caterpillars are worm-like creatures that change into moths or butterflies. They have soft bodies and many pairs of legs.

## cattle

Cattle are large animals, raised for their milk, meat, and skins. Cows and bulls are cattle.

## cauliflower

A cauliflower is a vegetable with a round, white head made of tiny flowers.

## cause

To cause something is to make it happen. Icy roads cause accidents.

## cautious

Cautious means very careful. You must be cautious before crossing a street. Be sure no traffic is coming.

## cave

A cave is a large hole in rock often big enough to walk in.

## ceiling

The ceiling is the inside top of a room. Mr. Impossible can walk on the ceiling. That's impossible!

## celebrate

To celebrate is to do something special because something special has happened. When Mr. Small got a new job he had a party to celebrate. Birthday celebrations are fun.

## cent

A cent is a piece of money. There are 100 cents in a dollar. A penny is one cent (1¢).

## center

The center of something is the middle of it.

A center is a main or important place, as in a shopping center or a central business area.

## cereal

A cereal is a plant with fruit called grains which we eat. Breakfast cereals, such as cornflakes and oatmeal, are made from these grains.

chain

ceiling

## chain

A chain is a string of rings joined together. Chains are used to pull, to connect, or to hang heavy objects.

chair

### chair
A chair is a seat for one person. Chairs have four legs, a seat, and a back.

### chalk
Chalk is a powdery stone made into the shape of a crayon. Chalk is used for writing on blackboards and for drawing.

### chance
The chance to do something is the time when it is possible to do it. Mr. Nosey took a chance. He looked in the mailbox while no one was home.

### change
To change is to become different. A caterpillar changes into a butterfly when it is fully grown.

To change also means to put on different clothes.

Change is money that you get back when you pay too much. If you give a dollar for a 75¢ book, you will get 25¢ change.

### charge
A charge is the amount of money asked for something when it is being sold. The grocer charged 50¢ for a bar of soap.

To charge is to make a bill for something that is being bought. The person takes the item and pays the bill later.

To charge a battery is to supply electricity.

To charge also means to rush at.

### chart
A chart is a drawing with information on it.

### chase
To chase is to run after and try to catch. Mr. Mischief took Mr. Grumpy's hat. Mr. Grumpy chased him all the way down the road to get it back.

### chatter
To chatter is to talk a lot. Mr. Chatterbox chatters to everyone, even himself!

### cheap
Cheap means not costing very much.

### cheat
To cheat is to do something that is unfair. Some people cheat at games.

a bull charging at Mr. Dizzy

Mr. Fussy is very careful to check his grocery bill before he pays it.

## check

When you check something, you make sure that it is right. Mr. Fussy checked his grocery bill three times before he paid it.

A check is a written order for money. Mr. Fussy paid his bill by writing a check.

## cheek

Your cheek is the part of your face between your nose and your ear.

cheek

## cheerful

Cheerful means happy. Little Miss Sunshine is always cheerful, but Mr. Grumpy never finds anything to be cheerful about.

## cheese

Cheese is a food made from milk. There are many different kinds of cheese.

## cherry

A cherry is a small, round, red fruit. Cherries grow on trees.

## chest

Your chest is the front part of your body between your neck and your waist. Your lungs and your heart are inside your chest.

A chest is a large strong box. Long ago, pirates hunted for treasure hidden in chests.

chest

## chew

To chew is to break up food with your teeth. It takes Mr. Slow all day to eat a raisin cookie because he chews each crumb and each raisin a hundred times.

chicken

## chicken
Chickens are birds that are kept on farms. They lay eggs and their meat can be cooked and eaten.

## chief
A chief is a leader, like an Indian chief. There are police and fire chiefs, too.

## child
A child is a young person. Boys and girls are children.

## chimney
A chimney is the part of a house built to let out smoke from a fireplace or furnace.

## chin
Your chin is the lowest part of your face. It is below your mouth and above your neck.

## china
China is the material that many plates and cups and saucers are made of. China is also the name given to these dishes.

## chip
A chip is a small piece of something. Little Miss Plump likes to eat potato chips.

To chip is to break off small pieces. Mr. Clumsy's cups are chipped because he drops them.

## chocolate
Chocolate is a flavoring made from cocoa beans. Mr. Greedy can never get enough chocolate candy or hot chocolate!

## choir
A choir is a group of people who sing together.

## choose
To choose is to pick something you want out of a group. Mr. Skinny chose the smallest cake. The largest cake was chosen by Mr. Greedy. Each one had his choice.

## chop
To chop is to cut something with quick action. An axe is used for chopping down trees.

To chop also means to cut into small pieces.

A chop is a piece of meat such as a pork chop or lamb chop.

## Christmas

Christmas Day is December 25th. It is the time when Christians celebrate the birth of Jesus.

## chuckle

To chuckle is to laugh quietly to yourself. Mr. Mischief chuckled when he thought about all the naughty things he had done.

## church

A church is a building where Christians go to pray and hear about God.

## circle

A circle is a perfect round flat shape. A ring is a circle.

To circle means to go around something.

## circus

A circus is a traveling show. At circuses you can see clowns, acrobats, and animals that do tricks.

## citizen

A citizen is a member of a city, state, or nation.

## city

A city is a large town. New York and London are large cities.

## claim

When you claim something, you say that it belongs to you or that it ought to belong to you.

## clap

To clap is to hit the palms of your hands together to make a loud noise. People clapped after the play to show that they were pleased.

## class

A class is a group of people or things that are alike.

A class is also a group of children who are taught together at school. Some teachers teach several classes every day.

circus

## claw

A claw is the sharp, hard point on the foot of an animal or bird. Cats use their claws to scratch.

## clay

Clay is a kind of soft earth that becomes hard when it is baked. Clay is used to make bricks. It can also be shaped into bowls and plates.

## clean

Clean means not dirty. After Mr. Messy had a bath, he looked cleaner than he had ever looked before.

## clear

To clear is to take or move something out of the way. The policeman cleared the traffic to let a fire engine go past.

Clear means bright and sunny, like a clear day.

Something that is clear can be seen through, like clear glass windows.

Also, something that is clear is simple and easy to understand. To be a good actor, you must speak clearly.

## clearing

A clearing is a place in a forest where there are no trees.

## clever

A clever person knows a lot and can do difficult things. Mr. Clever thinks he is the cleverest person ever.

## cliff

A cliff is a high wall of rock, usually close to the sea.

## climb

To climb is to go up something. Mr. Clumsy could never climb a tree without falling.

## cling

To cling means to hold on to something very tightly. Mr. Bounce clung to the edge of his chair to keep from bouncing up to the ceiling.

## clip

A clip is a small metal object used to hold things together. Paper clips fasten papers together.

To clip is to cut something shorter. You can use nail clippers when your nails are too long.

cliffs

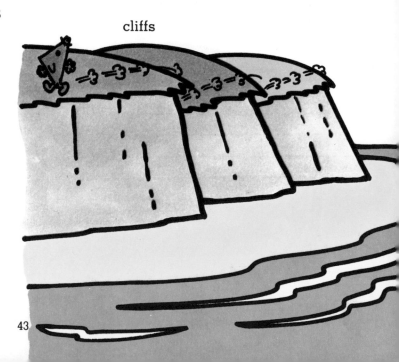

### clock

A clock is used to tell or measure time. It has a face with the numbers 1 to 12 around it, and two hands. The small hand shows what hour it is, and the big hand shows the minutes past the hour.

### close (It rhymes with dose.)

Close means near. Mr. Nonsense's house is close to Mr. Silly's. They live near each other.

### close (It rhymes with doze.)

To close means to shut. Mr. Sneeze closed the door of his house to keep out the cold.

### closet

A closet is a small room or cabinet or a closed place to keep things in.

### cloth

Cloth is a material made from thread-like cotton, wool and nylon. Sheets and curtains are some things made of cloth.

### clothes

Clothes are things that you wear. Dresses, shirts, shoes and jeans are clothes.

### cloud

A cloud is a collection of tiny drops of water that form a shape in the sky. Rain and snow fall from clouds.

### clown

A clown is a person who dresses up and does silly tricks to make people laugh.

### club

A club is a group of people who meet to do something together.

A club is also a heavy stick. Golf clubs have rounded heads at one end to hit golf balls.

### clue

A clue is a hint that helps you to find the answer to a puzzle.

### clumsy

Clumsy means careless or not able to be careful. A clumsy person is always knocking things over, bumping into things, or dropping things.

clock

Mr. Clumsy

## coach

To coach people means to help them be better at something. A football coach coaches the football team and helps them play better football.

## coal

Coal is a black mineral that is dug from under the ground by miners. When coal burns, it makes a bright, warm fire.

## coat

A coat is a covering. You wear a coat over your other clothes to keep warm.

## cocoa

Cocoa is a brown powder made from the seeds of the cocoa plant. It is used to make chocolate.

## coconut

A coconut is the fruit of a palm tree. Coconuts are large and have shells like wood. Inside there is white flesh and a white liquid, called coconut milk.

## code

A code is a set of symbols or words that stand for other words. Codes are used by spies for sending secret messages.

## coffee

Coffee is a drink made from the beans of a coffee tree.

## coin

A coin is a piece of money made of metal such as copper or silver. Nickels and dimes are coins.

## cold

Cold means not hot. Ice and snow are cold.

A cold is an illness that makes you sneeze.

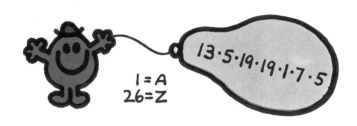

I = A
26 = Z

13·5·19·19·1·7·5

There is a word in code on Mr. Small's balloon. Can you work it out?

## collapse

To collapse means to fall down. Mr. Rush built a garden shed, in a hurry as usual. When the wind blew, the shed collapsed!

## collar

A collar goes around the neck of a person or animal. Shirts usually have collars.

collapse

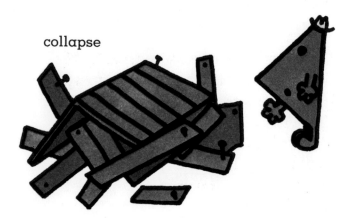

## collect

To collect means to gather together. Some people collect stamps as a hobby and keep their collection in albums.

## college

A college is a school after high school, for additional learning.

## collide

To collide means to bump into something with force. Two cars collided at the corner. Both were damaged because of the collision.

## color

Red, yellow and blue are colors. Green is the color of grass and white is the color of snow.

To color a picture is to put colors on it with crayons or paints.

## colossal

Colossal means very, very big. Mr. Greedy has a colossal appetite. He eats more for one meal than most people eat all day!

colors

## comb

A comb is used to make hair neat. It has a row of teeth along one edge.

## combine

To combine is to join things or to put things together. Apple pie and ice cream are a popular combination.

## come

To come is to go to a place. Mr. Happy invited his friends to come to a party at three o'clock. Everyone came on time but Little Miss Late.

To come also means to reach. Mr. Small doesn't even come up to Mr. Tall's belt.

## comfortable

To be comfortable is to feel at ease. A comfortable chair is pleasant to sit in. You are uncomfortable when you are cold, or unhappy, or in pain.

## comic

Something that is comic is funny. Comics are people who make you laugh. Comics are also pictures that tell a story. A funny show is called a comedy.

## command

To command is to order or direct someone to do something.

## company

Company means people together. Mr. Busy wanted company on his walk, so he invited Mr. Rush to go with him.

Company also means visitors.

A company is a group of people who work together.

## compete

To compete is to enter a contest or a race to find out who is best or first.

## complain

To complain is to grumble because you don't like something. Mr. Fussy complained that his bread was stale. He made a complaint to the bakery.

## complete

To complete means to finish. Mr. Rush never completes anything. He just rushes from one thing to the next.

Complete means having everything there. The jigsaw puzzle was complete. No pieces were missing.

Completely means totally. The cake was completely covered with chocolate.

Mr. Silly competed for the "Silliest Idea of the Year" and won the Nonsense Cup.

## compliment

A compliment is something good said to praise someone. If a person does good work, he likes to be complimented on it.

## computer

A computer is a machine that is used to solve problems and provide information at high speed.

computer

## concentrate

To concentrate means to pay close attention to what you are doing.

## concern

To concern means to have something to do with. Mr. Nosey is always prying into things that do not concern him.

Concerned means worried. Mr. Worry is concerned that Mr. Noisy might lose his voice because he shouts all the time.

## concert

A concert is a program of music for people to listen to.

## condition

The condition of something is the way it is. Little Miss Neat's house is in very good condition.

## conduct

Conduct is a way of acting. It is the way you behave.

To conduct is to be in charge or to direct, like the conductor on a train.

## confess

To confess is to admit that you have done something wrong; to make a confession.

## confide

To confide is to tell someone you trust something that you don't want anyone else to know. You have confidence in that person.

## confident

Confident means being sure. Mr. Rush was confident that he could run faster than Mr. Slow.

## confuse

To confuse is to mix up. Mr. Silly was confused when he saw a signpost in Nonsenseland. All the roads led nowhere! This sign always causes confusion.

confuse

## congratulate

To congratulate means to give good wishes to someone who has done something well or something special, like winning a race or getting married. You say, "Congratulations!" to that person.

## connect

To connect is to join things together. Where they join is called the connection.

## conservation

Conservation means saving or protecting something. Mr. Worry wants Mr. Forgetful to help conserve energy by remembering to turn out the lights when he leaves a room.

## consider

To consider something is to think about it carefully.

To be considerate is to be thoughtful and caring about other people. Mr. Mischief is not considerate when he plays tricks on people.

## consist

To consist of means to be made up of. A sewing kit consists of things like needles, pins, and scissors.

## constant

Constant means all the time. Mr. Worry's frown is constant because he worries so much.

## construct

To construct is to build by putting things together. Builders are sometimes called construction workers.

## contain

To contain means to hold or to have inside. Boxes, bottles, and bags are all containers.

## content

Content means pleased and happy. Mr. Greedy is only content after a big meal.

## contents

The contents of something are the things that are in it. The table of contents of a book is a list that tells what is in the book.

## contest

A contest is a game or a race that somebody tries to win. Mr. Strong and Mr. Happy had a contest to see who could lift the heaviest weight. Mr. Strong won, of course.

Mr. Topsy-Turvy could not control his airplane. He was flying all over the place.

contest

## continue

To continue is to keep on doing something. Mr. Chatterbox continued to talk even after everyone had gone away.

## contradict

To contradict someone is to say that person is wrong.

## control

To control something is to be in charge of it. A pilot must learn to control an airplane before he can fly.

Controls are instruments used for guiding machines.

## convenient

Convenient means useful or handy. A handkerchief is a convenient size for Mr. Small to use as a sheet for his bed.

## conversation

A conversation is people talking together.

## convict

To convict someone is to decide that he or she has done something wrong.

## convince

To convince someone of something is to make him believe it.

To be convinced is to be sure.

## cook
To cook is to make food ready to eat by using heat.

A cook is someone who cooks food.

## cookie
A cookie is a small crisp cake.

## cool
To cool something is to make it less hot.

Something cool is not too hot and not too cold.

## cooperate
To cooperate means to work with someone else in a helpful way. It is much easier to work as a team if everyone cooperates.

## copper
Copper is a metal that is red-brown in color. Pennies are made of copper.

## copy
To copy is to make something look the same as something else. There is a copying machine in the library.

A copy of something is exactly the same as the original. You can have copies of a photograph printed.

copy

## corn
Corn is a cereal with grains that grow on a holder called a corn cob. You can eat cooked corn directly from the cob. Corn is also made into cereal, as in cornflakes.

## corner
A corner is the place where lines or streets or walls meet. A square has four corners.

## correct
Correct means right. When someone asks Mr. Dizzy a question he never knows the correct answer.

To correct someone means to tell them the right answer or the right thing to do.

## corridor
A corridor is a long passage inside a building. Corridors usually have rooms on both sides.

## cost
The cost of something is the amount of money needed to buy it.

## costume
A costume is a particular kind of dress. When you go to a costume party, you may dress as a queen, or a cowboy, or a clown.

## cottage
A cottage is a small house. You usually find cottages in the country.

51

## cotton

Cotton is the thread or cloth made from the fluffy seeds of the cotton plant.

Cotton is also the fluffy white part of the cotton plant before it is made into thread or cloth.

## cough

A cough is a harsh noise that comes from the throat. You often have a cough with a cold.

## could

Could means to be able to.

## count

To count is to find out how many there are. Mr. Stingy spends hours counting his money.

To count on means to depend on or to be sure of someone or something.

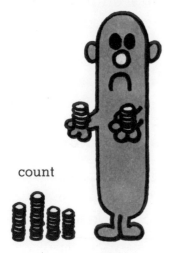

count

## counter

A counter is a long table in a store. The salesperson usually stands behind the counter.

A counter is also a work and storage area in the kitchen.

## country

A country is an area of land that has its own government. The United States and France and Spain are all different countries.

The country also means land outside towns and cities.

## couple

A couple means two things or people that go together. A married couple is a husband and wife.

## courage

Courage means someone is able to face unpleasant things without being afraid.

## course

A course is a group of lessons, like an English course.

A course is the act of moving from place to place in a special order.

Of course means surely.

## court

A tennis court is a piece of ground where tennis is played. A court of law is a place where one person or a group decides whether someone has broken a law.

The court is where a king or queen rules.

## cousin

Your cousin is the child of your aunt or uncle.

## cover

To cover something is to put something else over it to keep it clean, dry or warm.

cow

## cow

A cow is a female mammal. Cows eat grass and produce milk for us to drink.

## coward

A coward is a person who is not very brave. Sometimes cowards want to do something difficult or dangerous but are afraid to try.

## cowboy

A cowboy is a man who takes care of cattle on a ranch.

## crack

To crack is to break something a little bit but not into pieces. When Mr. Clumsy dropped a basket of eggs he cracked three and broke six.

A crack is a small, narrow opening or space between two things that are close together.

A crack is also a sudden sharp sound.

## cracker

A cracker is made of flour and baked in an oven. Crackers are flat and crisp.

## cradle

A cradle is a baby's bed that rocks.

## cramp

A cramp is a sharp pain in a muscle. You can get a cramp when you are swimming.

## crash

A crash is when two or more things collide with each other suddenly and with a loud noise.

## crawl

To crawl is to move along on your hands and knees.

The crawl is a stroke in swimming.

crawl

## crayon

A crayon is a stick of colored wax or chalk used to draw or write.

## crazy

Crazy means completely foolish or mad. Mr. Nonsense does crazy things. He uses his bed as a sled.

## cream

Cream is the thick part of milk with fat in it. Butter and cheese are made from cream.

## crease

A crease is a line or a mark made in paper or material when it is folded.

### create

To create means to make. Mr. Silly created a new dessert using milk, sugar and shoe polish.

### creature

A creature is any kind of animal. Fish are creatures that live in the sea.

### creep

To creep is to move slowly and quietly. Mr. Mischief crept around the side of Mr. Nervous's house to frighten him.

### crew

A crew is a team of people who work together. The crew of a boat or an airplane make it go and look after the passengers.

### crib

A crib is a baby's bed. It usually has sides on it to keep the baby from falling out.

### crime

A crime is a serious wrong act that is against the law.

### crisp

Crisp means hard but easily broken. Crackers are crisp when they are fresh.

### criticize

To criticize something is to say why you do or don't like it.

### crocodile

A crocodile is a large reptile that lives in water or on land near water. It has strong jaws with lots of sharp teeth.

### cross

To cross is to go from one side of something to another. Look carefully before you cross the road!

A cross is a mark like an X.

Cross also means rather angry. Mr. Grumpy is always cross about something.

crocodile

### crossroads

A crossroads is the place where two roads going in different directions pass over each other.

### crow

A crow is a large black bird. It makes a loud, sharp cry.

### crowd

A crowd is a large group of people. There were crowds of people enjoying themselves at the fair.

Crowded means full of people. It is hot and stuffy on a crowded bus.

crossroads

## crown

A crown is worn on the head by a king or queen. Crowns are usually made of gold and precious jewels.

## cruel

Cruel means very unkind. It is cruel to pull a dog's tail. It is painful for the dog.

## crumb

A crumb is a very small piece of bread or cake. Mr. Messy always drops crumbs on the table when he eats.

crown

## crunch

To crunch something is to break it noisily. You make a crunching noise when you eat potato chips.

## crush

To crush is to squeeze or mash something.

## crust

The crust is the crisp, outside part of a loaf of bread. Mr. Fussy always cuts the crusts off his sandwiches.

## cry

When you cry, tears come out of your eyes because you are unhappy or in pain. The little girl was crying when she fell off her swing.

To cry also means to shout. Little Miss Bossy cried, "Careful, Mr. Bump!" when she saw him climbing a tree.

## cuckoo

A cuckoo is a bird that lays its eggs in other birds' nests. When the cuckoo calls, it says, "Cuckoo."

## cucumber

A cucumber is a long, green salad vegetable.

## cunning

Cunning means being clever at fooling people. Mr. Mischief is cunning. He is always playing tricks on people and nobody ever catches him.

## cup

A cup is a container used to drink from.

A cup is also a measurement used in cooking.

## cupboard

A cupboard is a closet or a piece of furniture with shelves inside. It is used to store things like food and cups and plates.

This pig has a curly tail.

cupboard

## cure

To cure a sick person or animal means to make him well again.

## curious

Curious means wanting to know about something. Mr. Nosey is curious about everything.

Curious also means strange or unusual. Little Miss Shy heard a curious squeaking noise outside. It was only the branch of a tree blowing in the wind.

## curl

To curl is to twist into a curved shape. Some people have naturally curly hair.

## current

A current is the way something flows, such as the movement of air or of water in a river.

Current is also the amount of movement of electricity.

Current means now. Something that is happening currently is happening at the present time.

## curtain

A curtain is made from material and hung at a window. You open the curtains to let in light.

## curve

A curve is a line that bends.

## cushion

A cushion is a soft pad put on a seat to make it more comfortable or higher.

## customer

A customer is a person who buys something.

## cut

To cut is to make a slit in something or make it into separate pieces with a sharp instrument like a knife or scissors. Mr. Fussy cuts his grass one blade at a time.

## cute

Cute means little and pretty. Puppies are cute.

### dad, daddy
Dad and daddy are names that people call their fathers.

### daily
Daily means happening every day. Mr. Busy cleans his house daily.

### dairy
A dairy is a place where milk and cream are kept and made into butter and cheese.

### daisy
A daisy is a small flower with a yellow center and white petals.

### damage
To damage means to break something or stop it from working properly. Mr. Clumsy damaged his clock when he dropped it.

### damp
Damp means slightly wet. In the early morning the dew makes the grass damp.

### dance
To dance is to move around in time to music. People dance to music at parties. Dancing is fun.

### dandelion
A dandelion is a bright, yellow flower; a weed that grows in the garden.

### dangerous
Something that is dangerous is likely to hurt people. Broken glass is dangerous. You can cut yourself on it.

### dare
To dare is to be brave enough to do something. Mr. Nervous heard a strange noise but he did not dare go and see what it was.

dark

## dark
Dark means having no light. It is very dark at night when there is no moon.

## date
The date is a particular day of the month. The date of Christmas Day is December 25th.

A date is also a time and place to meet someone.

Another kind of date is a sweet, sticky fruit.

## daughter
A daughter is a female child.

## dawn
Dawn is the beginning of daylight in the morning.

## day
A day is 24 hours long, counting from one midnight to the next midnight.

Day is the time between sunrise and sunset.

## daydream
To daydream is to dream while you are awake. You think you are somewhere else doing something different. Mr. Daydream always daydreams about adventure.

## daze
To daze is to make someone dizzy or confused. Mr. Bump was dazed after he hit his head on a lamp post.

## dead
Dead means no longer alive. The dog was dead. His death was caused by a speeding car.

## deaf
Deaf means not able to hear. Deaf people learn to understand others by watching their lips move and by using sign language.

## dear
Dear means much loved or highly thought of.

## decide
To decide is to make up your mind. Mr. Greedy could not decide whether to buy a chocolate cake or a cream pie. It was a hard decision to make.

## decorate
To decorate something means to make it look pretty. Mr. Chatterbox had a birthday cake decorated with icing and candles.

a decorated cake

deep

## deed

A deed is an action, especially a good or a brave action.

A deed is also a legal agreement. Mr. Happy signed the deed for his new house.

## deep

Deep means going down a long way. Diving into deep water is fun, as long as you are a good swimmer. The depth of water is how deep it is.

## deer

A deer is a mammal that lives in forests. Male deer have horns called antlers.

## definite

Definite means certain. Mr. Happy has not made definite plans for his vacation.

## delay

To delay is to make late. In winter, the school bus is often delayed because of ice and snow.

To delay also means to put off to a later time.

## deliberately

Deliberately means on purpose. Mr. Mischief deliberately bumped into Mr. Fussy and made him drop his shopping basket.

## delicious

Delicious means good to eat or to smell.

## delight

To delight is to give pleasure. Mr. Happy was delighted to see the sunshine. It was a delightful day.

## deliver

To deliver is to carry something and give it to someone. The letter carrier delivers letters, cards and packages.

## den

A den is the home of a wild animal, like a fox's den.

A den is also a room to read and relax in.

## dentist

A dentist is a person who looks after people's teeth.

dentist

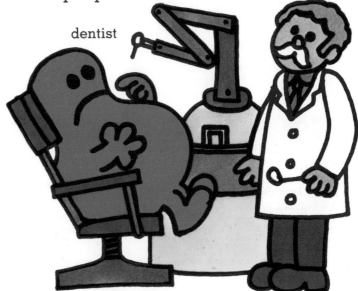

### department

A department is a part of a school, or an office, or a store. A department store has different departments to sell shoes, toys, books and other things.

### depend

To depend on means to rely on, to need something from someone. Young animals are dependent on their parents for food.

Depend also means to be influenced by. We may have a picnic tomorrow. It depends on the weather.

### describe

To describe something means to say what it is like, to give a description of it.

### desert

A desert is a hot, dry, sandy area of land with few plants growing on it. Very little water is found in the desert.

### deserted

Deserted means completely empty. The streets are deserted during a storm. Everyone stays inside to keep dry.

### deserve

To deserve means to have a right to. Mr. Lazy felt that he deserved a rest after spending a whole five minutes working in his garden.

### design

To design something means to draw or make a plan of how you are going to make it. Airplane designers draw designs before they start building new planes.

### desire

To desire is to wish for or to want something. A desire is a strong feeling of wanting something.

### desk

A desk is a piece of furniture that you work at. It has a flat top where you can read, write or draw. It usually has drawers for keeping papers and pens.

desk

### dessert

A dessert is the last part of a meal. Popular desserts are cakes, pies, fruit and ice cream.

desert

## destroy

To destroy means to ruin completely. Fire destroyed a whole row of buildings.

## detail

A detail is a very small part of something. The artist drew a picture of the candy store in detail. He drew every single jar with all the candies inside!

detective

## detective

A detective is a person who looks for information so that crimes can be solved.

## detest

To detest something is to hate it very much.

## dew

The small drops of water found on grass early in the morning are called dew.

## dial

A dial is the front of a telephone that is marked with numbers. To dial a number on the telephone you put your finger on the number you want and move the dial around.

dial

## diamond

A diamond is a precious stone that is clear like glass and sparkles.

A diamond is also a 4-sided shape ◆. Baseball is played on a field marked off in the shape of a diamond.

## diary

A diary is a book with a space for each day of the year. In a diary you write down the things you do each day.

## dictionary

A dictionary is a book that tells you what words mean and how they are used and spelled. This book is a dictionary.

## die

To die is to stop living. Plants and animals die if they cannot get enough water. In autumn dead leaves fall from trees.

## diet

A diet is the food we eat.

To diet is to eat less food. People who are fat sometimes diet to help them get thinner.

## different

Different means not the same. Mr. Happy and Mr. Grumpy are really different.

## difficult
Difficult means not easy. It is difficult for Mr. Lazy to stay awake.

## dig
To dig means to make a hole in the ground. Mr. Topsy-Turvy is digging a hole in the garden with his shovel upside down. He will never get it dug that way!

## dime
A dime is a coin that is worth ten cents.

## dip
To dip is to put something into a liquid for a moment and take it out again. Mr. Silly dipped a finger into his lemonade to make sure it was wet!

## direction
A direction is an order, telling how something should be done. The actors followed directions. They did what the director told them to do.

The direction of something is the way to get to it. Mr. Wrong started to go to the grocery store, but he went in the wrong direction.

## dirty
Dirty means not clean. Mr. Messy's house is always dirty because he never cleans it.

## disagree
To disagree means to think differently about something. Mr. Grumpy and Mr. Happy always disagree about things.

dig

## dinner
Dinner is the main meal of the day. People usually eat meat and vegetables for dinner.

## dinosaur
A dinosaur was a very large reptile that lived millions of years ago.

dinosaur

Mr. Impossible disappearing.

## disappear

To disappear means to go out of sight. Mr. Greedy can make food disappear faster than anyone.

## disappoint

To disappoint someone is to fail to do what that person expected or wanted to happen. Mr. Greedy was disappointed when he found the bakery closed earlier than usual.

## disapprove

To disapprove of something means to think it is not right, or not good. Mr. Busy disapproves of Mr. Lazy staying in bed until noon.

## disaster

A disaster is something terrible that happens suddenly, like a plane crash or an earthquake.

## discover

To discover means to learn or find something for the first time. Mr. Happy helped Mr. Miserable discover how to smile. What a discovery!

## discuss

To discuss is to talk things over with other people. The people of Tiddletown had a discussion about Mr. Nosey and his nosey ways.

## disease

A disease is an illness. Measles is a disease that many children get.

## disgrace

A disgrace is a shame. It is something not pleasant or not right. Mr. Messy's house is a disgrace.

## disguise

To disguise yourself is to change the way you look so that other people won't know who you are. Mr. Chatterbox tried to disguise himself by wearing a false moustache. Everyone knew it was Mr. Chatterbox in disguise because he talked so much!

## disgust

Disgust is a feeling of being shocked by something. Bullying smaller children is a disgusting way to behave.

disguise

### dish

A dish is a plate used for eating or serving food. Mr. Messy only washes his dishes when he has no more clean ones to use.

### disobey

To disobey is not to do what you are told. Then, you are disobedient.

### distance

The distance between two places or things is how far apart they are.

In the distance means far away. As the train came around the bend, the passengers could see a lake in the distance.

### disturb

To disturb means to interrupt. Mr. Lazy was asleep when the sound of the telephone disturbed him. After the disturbance, he went back to sleep.

### ditch

A ditch is a long, narrow hole in the ground. There is a ditch next to most country roads for rain water to drain into.

### dive

To dive is to go into water head first. Diving is fun.

### divide

To divide something is to make it into parts.

### dizzy

Dizzy means feeling as if you are going to fall over. You feel dizzy after you spin around and around very quickly.

Dizzy also means not thinking clearly, being confused or foolish.

distance

doctor

## do

To do is to act or to make something happen. Mr. Lazy hates doing anything. He did wash one plate after breakfast. He never gets any job done. He only does a little at a time.

## doctor

A doctor is a person who takes care of your health and treats people who are sick or hurt.

## dog

A dog is a mammal. Dogs are kept as pets or as guard or hunting dogs.

## doll

A doll is a toy that resembles a person.

## dollar

A dollar is money that is worth 100 cents. A dollar bill is paper money. There is also a one dollar coin.

## dolphin

A dolphin is a mammal that looks like a fish and lives in the sea. Dolphins are playful and can be taught to do tricks.

## donkey

A donkey is an animal with long ears that looks like a small horse.

## door

A door opens or shuts an opening into a room or a building. A doorway is where a door is.

## dot

A dot is a small round spot. The dot at the end of a sentence is called a period.

## double

Double means twice as big or twice as much. Two people sleep in a double bed but only one person sleeps in a single bed.

## doubtful

Doubtful means not sure about something. Mr. Happy thought it was warm enough to go for a swim, but Mr. Worry was doubtful. He thought it would be too cold.

doughnut

## dough

Dough is a mixture of flour and water or milk used to bake bread or cake. A doughnut is a small round cake that usually has a hole in the middle.

## down

Down means going from higher to lower. It is fun to slide down a hill on a sled.

## downstairs

Downstairs means going from the top of the stairs to the bottom. Mr. Clumsy is always tripping over his shoelaces and falling downstairs.

downstairs

## draft

A draft is cold air that blows through a crack in a window or under a door. It is not pleasant to be in a drafty place.

## drag

To drag means to pull heavy things. Mr. Slow helped Mr. Skinny drag a table across the room.

## dragon

A dragon is an animal that is only found in stories. Dragons have large scaly bodies and breathe fire.

dragon

## drain

To drain is to take away a little at a time.

A drain is an opening for things to go through, like the drain in a bathtub to let the water out.

## draw

To draw is to make a picture with a pencil, a pen or a crayon. Mr. Clever drew a picture of Mr. Small.

A drawing is a picture that has been drawn by someone.

To draw is also to pull, as a horse drawn wagon.

## drawer

A drawer is a long, flat box without a top that fits into a piece of furniture. Drawers have handles so they can be pulled out and pushed in.

## dreadful

Dreadful means very bad. Mr. Grumpy tore all the pages out of his book. It was a dreadful thing to do.

## dream

To dream is to think of things while you are asleep. Mr. Lazy dreamed that he had to go for a long walk. He was very pleased when he found it was only a dream.

dream

## dress

To dress is to put on clothes.

A dress has a skirt and a top all in one piece. Women and girls wear dresses.

## drill

To drill is to do something again and again so you can do it the right way.

A drill is a tool used for making holes.

## drink

To drink is to swallow liquid. Mr. Rush was very thirsty after running around. He drank three glasses of lemonade before rushing off again.

## drip

To drip is to fall in drops. The sound of water dripping can keep Mr. Quiet awake all night.

drive

## drive

To drive is to make something move along by guiding it. When Mr. Bump got his first car he drove straight into a lamp post. He had never driven before!

To drive also means to hit, like driving a nail into wood.

## droop

To droop is to hang down sadly. After two weeks without rain, the flowers in the garden drooped.

drooping flowers

## drop

To drop something is to let it fall. Mr. Clumsy dropped a plate full of beans and made a terrible mess.

A drop is a tiny ball of liquid. Rain falls in drops from the sky.

## drought

A drought is a long time without rain.

## drown

To drown is to die under water because you cannot breathe.

## drum

A drum is a musical instrument that makes a thumping noise when you hit it with your hand or a stick.

ducks

drums

## dry

Dry means not wet.

To dry something means to make it dry. Mr. Clumsy dried his hair after a walk in the rain.

## duck

A duck is a bird that can swim. Ducks have webbed feet so that they can swim in rivers and lakes.

To duck is to bend out of the way. Mr. Tall had to duck his head to go into Mr. Small's house.

## during

During means within a period of time. Many people take their vacations during the summer.

## dust

Dust is very tiny bits of dirt. You can sometimes see dust on furniture. There is never a speck of dust at Mr. Fussy's house. He even dusts his flowers!

## dwarf

A dwarf is a very small person.

## dwell

To dwell in a place means to live or to stay there.

Mr. Fussy is dusting his flowers!

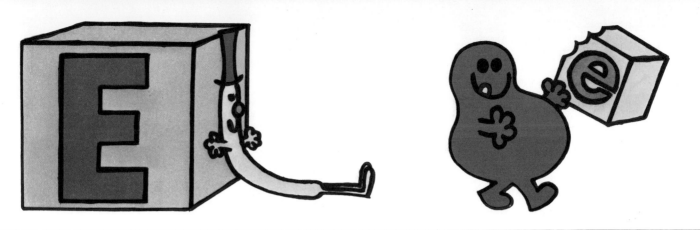

## each

Each means everyone. There is a story about each of the Mr. Men and Little Misses.

## eagle

An eagle is a large powerful bird, often used as a symbol of the United States.

## ear

You have two ears, one on each side of your head. Your ears help you to hear.

## early

Early means before the right time. Mr. Worry was worried that he would be late for the party. So he arrived two hours early!

Early also means first thing in the morning. Mr. Lazy doesn't like to get up early.

## earn

To earn something is to get it by working for it. Mr. Rush tried to find a job so that he could earn enough money for a vacation.

## earth

We live on a planet called earth. It is a huge round body that moves around the sun.

Earth is also another word for soil. We plant flowers in the earth.

## earthquake

An earthquake is a movement of the earth's surface that makes the ground shake.

## east

East is a direction. The sun rises in the east. New York City is in the eastern part of the United States.

## easy

Something that is easy is not hard to do. Some puzzles are easier to do than others. Mr. Clever can solve most puzzles easily.

earth

## eat

To eat is to take food into the mouth, chew it, and swallow it. Mr. Greedy ate his dinner early. Before he went to bed he had eaten two chocolate cakes and four packages of cookies!

## echo

An echo is the same sound coming back again. If you shout in a cave you will hear echoes of your own voice coming back a few seconds later.

## edge

The edge of something is the place where it ends. A knife has a sharp edge.

## effort

When you make an effort you try very hard to do something. It takes a lot of effort to lift heavy things.

## egg

We eat eggs that have been laid by hens. Birds, fish, and reptiles lay eggs. Baby animals grow from eggs.

## either

Either means one or the other of two. You are either a boy or a girl, but you are not both.

## elbow

Your elbow is the part of your arm that bends.

elbow

## electricity

Electricity is a kind of power. Light bulbs, washing machines and televisions need electricity to make them work.

Electric means using electricity. Electric trains run on electricity.

## elephant

An elephant is a very large heavy mammal with a long trunk and large ears.

## elevator

An elevator is a small room or a platform that moves up and down in tall buildings.

elephant

## else

Else means someone or something more than the one mentioned.

70

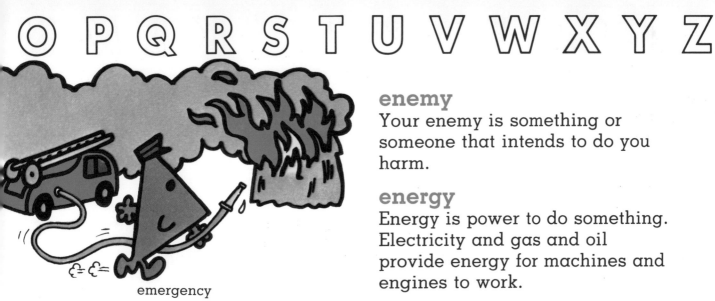

emergency

## embarrassed

When you are embarrassed you feel silly and uncomfortable about yourself.

## emergency

An emergency is something serious that happens without warning. House fires and road accidents are emergencies.

## empty

Something that is empty has nothing inside it. Mr. Skinny's shelves are usually empty.

To empty something is to take everything out of it.

## encourage

To encourage means to give someone courage and helpful advice. Mr. Happy encouraged Mr. Clever to enter the quiz contest. He thought Mr. Clever could win it.

## end

The end is the last part of something. At the end of the play, the audience clapped loudly.

To end means to finish.

## enemy

Your enemy is something or someone that intends to do you harm.

## energy

Energy is power to do something. Electricity and gas and oil provide energy for machines and engines to work.

## engine

An engine is the part of a car or train or plane that makes it move. Engines work by burning oil or gas or by using electricity. An engineer operates a railroad engine.

enjoy

## enjoy

To enjoy something is to like doing it. Mr. Tickle enjoys tickling people, but not everyone enjoys being tickled.

## enormous

Enormous means very, very big. Mr. Greedy has an enormous appetite.

## enough

Enough means as much as is needed. Mr. Skinny bought only one carrot. He said it would be enough for lunch.

### enter
To enter is to go in. Everyone laughed when Mr. Topsy-Turvy entered the room backwards.

### entertain
To entertain is to help someone spend time pleasantly. Actors, dancers and singers are entertainers. Movies, plays, and games are different kinds of entertainment.

### envelope
An envelope is a paper holder. You put a letter in an envelope before you mail it.

### envy
To envy is to think someone is luckier than you. Everybody envied Little Miss Neat when she was given a new bicycle for Christmas.

### equipment
Equipment is special items required to do a job or play a game.

### erase
To erase something is to wipe it away. An eraser on a pencil wipes away pencil marks.

### errand
An errand is a short trip for a purpose. Mr. Skinny went on an errand for Little Miss Plump to get a loaf of bread.

escalator

equal

### equal
Equal means exactly the same. Mr. Silly and Mr. Nonsense are sharing the cake equally.

### error
An error is a mistake. Mr. Uppity complained because there was an error in his bill.

### escalator
An escalator is a moving staircase.

## escape

To escape is to get away. Mr. Mischief escaped from Mr. Busy by running as fast as he could.

## essential

Essential means important or necessary. It is essential to brush your teeth every day to keep them clean and healthy.

## even

An even number can be divided by two. Six and ten are even numbers; three and seven are odd numbers.

Even also means the same. At half-time in the football game the score was even. Both teams had the same score.

Even can mean more so. Jane is a good reader, but John is even better.

Even means flat and level. Mr. Slow made the bumpy road even by driving a steamroller over it.

making a road even

## evening

The part of the day between afternoon and night is called evening. In the evening it begins to get dark.

## event

An event is anything that happens, especially something important. Landing on the moon was an important event.

## eventually

Eventually means at last. The farmer tried for a long time to push his tractor. Eventually, with Mr. Strong's help, he moved it.

## ever

Ever means always. Mr. Happy enjoyed the beach so much, he wished he could stay there forever.

Ever also means at any time. Has Mr. Greedy ever had enough to eat?

## every

Every means all. Mr. Worry wrote down every problem that worried him. It was a very long list! He worries about everything and everybody.

## exact

Exact means absolutely right. Mr. Clever was very pleased with the new books. They were exactly what he wanted.

### exaggerate

To exaggerate is to say that something is bigger or better than it really is. When it thundered, Mr Nervous said it sounded like an earthquake. He always exaggerates.

### examine

To examine is to inspect or test. When you go to the doctor, he examines you to see if you are healthy.

An examination, or exam, is a test given to question what you know.

### example

You use an example to show what something is like. An example of Mr. Mischief's idea of fun is the time he cut off half of Mr. Fussy's moustache.

### excellent

Excellent means very, very good. When your teacher says that your work is excellent, you can be pleased.

### except

Except means all but. None of the Mr. Men here is wearing a scarf, except Mr. Snow.

### exciting

Exciting means thrilling and enjoyable. Mr. Daydream likes to dream of exciting adventures.

### excuse

When you excuse someone for a mistake or a wrongdoing, you let that person off without blame or punishment. Mr. Happy excused Mr. Slow for being late.

An excuse is a reason. Whenever Mr. Lazy is late, his excuse is that he fell asleep.

except

expecting rain

## expect

To expect is to wait for something that you believe is going to happen.

## expensive

Expensive means costing a lot of money. Mr. Uppity is very rich. He buys expensive clothes and cars.

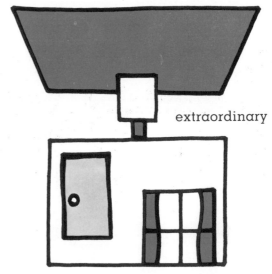

extraordinary

## exercise

Exercise means practice or activity that keeps you fit. Mr. Rush gets plenty of exercise rushing around all day.

## exhausted

Exhausted means very tired. Mr. Small was exhausted after his walk home from the beach. All he wanted to do was sleep.

## exhibit

To exhibit is to show. Artists exhibit art at an art show. The show is called an exhibition.

## exist

To exist is to be alive or real. Some people believe that ghosts exist.

## exit

An exit is a way to go out.

## extra

Extra means more than enough or more than usual.

## extraordinary

Extraordinary means very strange or unusual. Mr. Muddle's house is extraordinary.

## eye

An eye is the part of your body that you see with. When you close your eyes, you cover them with your eyelids. Above each eye is a curve of small hairs called an eyebrow.

## face

Your face is the front part of your head. On your face you have two eyes, a nose, a mouth, and a chin.

To face something is to look towards it. Mr. Quiet is facing Mr. Small at the table.

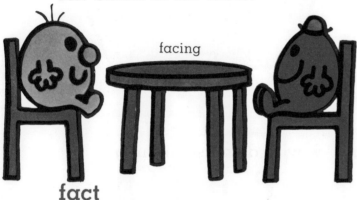

facing

## fact

A fact is something real and true. It is a fact that dogs and cats are animals.

## factory

A factory is a large building where things are made. Cars and clothing are made in factories.

## fade

To fade is to become pale or lose color. Blue jeans fade after a lot of washing.

## fail

To fail is not to be successful or not to do enough. Mr. Topsy-Turvy's flowers failed to bloom because he planted them upside down.

## faint

To faint is to feel weak and dizzy. When a person faints he falls over and seems to sleep.

Faint also means weak or not clear. The ink in old books is sometimes too faint to read.

## fair

Fair means right or reasonable. It is not fair for Mr. Greedy to have all the cakes when Mr. Skinny has not had any.

Fair also means light in color.

Fair weather is clear, not cloudy.

A fair is a place where you can have fun with games and rides.

Fair means neither very good nor very bad.

## fairy

A fairy is a creature found in stories. Fairies are usually small and have magic powers.

fair

## fall

To fall is to drop to a lower place. Mr. Bump went for a walk on an icy day and fell over twice before he reached the gate! By the time he got to the corner he had fallen eight times.

Fall is another name for autumn, the season between summer and winter.

## false

False means not real or not true. A lie is a false statement.

## family

A family is a group of people who are related. Your family includes your parents, brothers and sisters, cousins, aunts and uncles and grandparents.

## famous

Famous means well-known. A crowd gathered to see the famous television star.

## fan

A fan is used to move air around, usually for cooling.

A fan is also a person who likes a particular sport, such as a baseball fan.

## far

Far means a long way. Mr. Lazy does not like to walk very far.

farm

## farm

A farm is land where animals such as cows and pigs are kept. Foods like corn and vegetables are grown on farms.

A farmer is a person who owns or runs a farm.

## fashion

Fashion means a style of clothes or a way of doing something.

## fast

Fast means moving at great speed. Mr. Rush moves so fast that no one can keep up with him.

To fast also means not to eat.

## fasten

To fasten something is to close it or to attach it to something else. Mr. Messy never fastens the gate. It blows in the wind.

## fat

Fat means big all over. Mr. Greedy is fat because he eats too much.

Fat is also part of meat. It can be used for cooking.

## father

A father is a man who has children.

## fault

If something is a person's fault, it means that he or she is to blame for what happened. Mr. Tickle tickled Mr. Dizzy and made him drop a plate. It was Mr. Tickle's fault that the plate was broken.

## favorite

Your favorite is the one you like the best. Mr. Lazy's favorite way of spending an afternoon is sleeping.

## fear

Fear is a feeling of being very frightened or in danger. Mr. Nervous trembles with fear every time he hears a strange noise.

## feast

A feast is a large meal for a special occasion. Mr. Greedy dreamed that he was invited to a great feast with every kind of food he could think of.

## feather

feathers

Feathers grow on birds to keep them warm and dry. Feathers are light and fluffy.

## feed

To feed is to give food. Mr. Muddle was feeding his neighbor's pets while they were away. He fed birdseed to the cat and catfood to the parrot!

feed

feast

## feel

To feel is to touch something and know that you have touched it. A kitten feels soft and warm.

To feel also means how you are. Mr. Dizzy felt upset because everyone laughed at his mistakes. Happiness and anger and fear and worry are all feelings.

## female

A female is one who gives birth to young. A female person is a girl or a woman. Some female animals are hens, mares and cows.

## fence

A fence is a row of posts or boards or wires. It marks the edge of a piece of ground, such as a garden or a playground.

## ferry

A ferry is a boat used to carry people or goods across a narrow stretch of water. Mr. Slow likes traveling on a ferry boat because it goes so slowly.

## fever

A fever is a rise in body temperature. When you have a fever, you feel sick.

ferry

## few

A few means a small number or not many. By the time Mr. Greedy had done his shopping at the bakery, there were only a few cookies left!

## field

A field is a large piece of land. A farmer usually has several fields where he grows plants and keeps cows and sheep.

## fierce

Fierce means violent or very angry. A fierce animal is one that is likely to attack people.

## fight

A fight is a battle or an argument.

To fight means to hurt a person by hitting or saying something to hurt him or her. Mr. Happy has never fought with anyone.

fierce

## figure

A figure is a written number; 3 and 5 are figures.

A figure is the form or shape of something, like a person or a circle or a square.

To figure is to work with numbers or ideas to get answers.

## fill

To fill means to put something into a container until there is no more room inside. Mr. Greedy filled his cupboard with cakes. After it was full, he ate the doughnuts with cream filling!

film

## film

A film is a story told in moving pictures. Mr. Funny likes watching cartoon films.

Film is the thin strip of material that you put into a camera to take photographs.

## filthy

Filthy means very dirty. Mr. Fussy doesn't like to work in the garden. A little dirt makes him feel filthy.

## finally

Finally means in the end or at last. After spending a long time with Mr. Happy, Mr. Miserable finally learned how to smile.

## finances

Finances mean money or the management of money.

## find

To find means to come upon something or to go and get something. Mr. Forgetful couldn't find his hat anywhere. He finally found it on his head!

## fine

Fine means well or good or excellent. Mr. Neat and Mr. Tidy did a fine job cleaning Mr. Messy's house.

Fine also means very thin or small, as in fine sand.

A fine is a sum of money paid as a punishment.

## finger

Your fingers are at the end of your hands. People have four fingers and a thumb on each hand. Mr. Men only have three!

## finish

To finish means to bring to an end.

sore finger

## fire

Fire is the heat and light given off by something that is burning. A fireman's job is to put out fires that are dangerous.

To fire a gun is to shoot it.

To fire a person is to tell her or him to leave a job.

## firm

Firm means solid and not easily moved. Mr. Clever made sure that the chair was firm and steady before he stood on it.

A firm is a business.

## first

First means before all the others. The first letter in the alphabet is A.

fish

## fish

Fish are cold-blooded animals that live in water. To fish is to hunt for fish. Mr. Clumsy fell out of the boat when he went fishing.

## fit

To fit is to be the right size and shape. Mr. Funny's new hat didn't fit very well. It came down over his eyes.

To be fit means to be well and strong.

## fix

To fix means to mend or to put together. Mr. Clever fixed the alarm clock after he had dropped it on the floor.

## flag

A flag is a piece of cloth that can be fixed to a pole. Flags have different colors or designs to show that they belong to a country or a group.

## flame

A flame is fire that shoots up when something is burning. Flames leap up around logs in a campfire.

## flash

A flash is a sudden bright light. After a flash of lightning, thunder soon follows.

## flat

A flat surface is smooth and level. Where the countryside is flat, there are no hills.

## flavor

A flavor is a taste. Ice cream is made in many flavors.

## flea

A flea is a tiny insect. Fleas live on dogs and other animals.

## flee

To flee is to run away. The thief fled when he saw a policeman.

## flight

Flight is the ability to fly.

A flight is a trip on an airplane.

A flight is also a group of steps.

flags

float

## float

To float means to stay on the top of a liquid without sinking. Wood floats on water, but stones sink to the bottom.

To float also means to move gently through the air. When you drop a feather, it floats slowly to the ground.

## flood

To flood is to fill with too much liquid. After heavy rains, the river overflowed and flooded the city.

## floor

The floor is the part of a room that you walk on.

A floor is also a level of a building. Office buildings can have many floors.

## flour

Flour is a soft white or brown powder that is made from ground grain. Flour is used to make breads and cakes.

## flow

To flow is to move along in a stream, like a river.

flowers

## flower

A flower is the blossom of a plant or tree. Most flowers have petals and are colorful.

## fluffy

Fluffy means covered with soft, light hairs or feathers. Some baby animals are fluffy.

## fly

To fly is to move through the air. Mr. Daydream dreamed that he flew across the country, but he has never really flown at all.

A fly is an insect that flies.

## foam

Foam is a lot of bubbles all together. Some soaps make foam when you swish them around in water.

foam

fog

## foot

Your foot is the part of your body at the end of your leg. You have two feet to stand on.

The foot means the bottom of something. Mr. Small hangs his hat at the foot of his bed.

A foot is also a measurement. A foot is 12 inches.

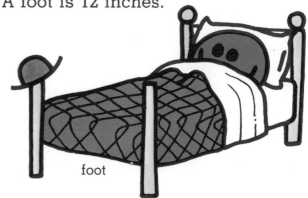

foot

## fog

Fog is a cloud that has come down to the ground. Fog makes everything look misty. When it is foggy, it is hard to see very far.

## fold

To fold something is to make it smaller by bending one part of it on to another part. Mr. Fussy always folds his clothes neatly before he puts them away.

## follow

To follow means to go or to come after something else. Mr. Wrong follows Mr. Right so he won't get lost.

## fond

Fond means liking very much. Mr. Mischief is fond of playing tricks on people.

## food

Food is what is eaten. Mr. Greedy never gets enough food to eat.

## foolish

Foolish means not sensible. It is foolish to go out in the snow without boots.

## for

For means with a purpose. This dictionary is for children.

For also means in order to. It takes a long time for Mr. Lazy to do things.

For can mean during a time. Mr. Lazy has been asleep for a week.

For means giving or getting something in return. Pencils cost 25¢ for three.

## force

Force is strength or power. Mr. Strong used force to open the locked door.

To force means to make someone do something.

## forehead

Your forehead is the part of your face above your eyes.

## foreign
Foreign means coming from a different country. Some people collect foreign coins as a hobby.

## forest
A forest is a large area of land covered with trees.

## forget
Forget means not remember. Mr. Forgetful forgot to take money with him to the store, but it didn't matter. He had forgotten what he wanted to buy!

## forgive
To forgive is to excuse someone for saying or doing something against you. You forgive him or her and are friends again. Mr. Fussy forgave Mr. Mischief for playing a trick on him.

fork

A fork has three or four points at one end. You use a fork to put food into your mouth.

## form
Form is shape or appearance. To form something is to make it into a definite shape.

## fortunately
Fortunately means luckily. It started to rain as Mr. Happy walked home from shopping. Fortunately, he had just bought a new umbrella.

## fortune
A fortune is a large sum of money. To make a fortune, you have to work very hard or be very lucky.

Your fortune also means what will happen to you in the future.

## forward
Forward means facing front. When you walk forward you are going to a place in front of you.

## fountain
A fountain is a structure that shoots water into the air. You can take a drink of water at a drinking fountain.

## fowl
Fowl are birds. Chickens, ducks and turkeys are fowl.

fox

## fox
A fox is a wild animal that looks like a small dog. Foxes have thick fur, long pointed noses, and bushy tails. Farmers do not like foxes because they steal chickens.

frame

## frame

A frame is what you put around a picture.

A frame is also the shape of something.

## free

Free means not costing anything. Some people go to see a show only if it is free.

Free also means able to move around as you please. Freedom is being able to act without being told what to do.

## freeze

To freeze is to become hard or solid because of the cold. One winter morning Mr. Sneeze found his milk frozen in the bottle. The weather was so cold that the milk froze.

## fresh

Fresh means new and not old or stale. Fresh air is usually cool and clear.

Fresh also means not polite.

## friend

A friend is someone you like and can trust. Mr. Silly and Mr. Nonsense are great friends. Their friendship has lasted a long time.

## fright

A fright is a sudden fear.

To frighten is to cause sudden fear. Mr. Mischief frightened Mr. Nervous by jumping out from behind a wall.

## frog

A frog is a small jumping animal, an amphibian that has no tail.

## from

From means where something begins. Mr. Silly got a letter from Mr. Nonsense.

From also means distance or difference between things. Mr. Nonsense lives a block from Mr. Silly. If you take away three from five, you have two left.

frown

## front

The front of something is the first part or the part that faces forward. Mr. Small has to sit in the front row at the theater so that he can see the show.

## frown

To frown is to wrinkle your forehead. You frown when you are angry or worried or thinking hard. Mr. Worry always frowns.

further

## fruit

A fruit is the part of a plant or tree that holds the seeds. Many kinds of fruit are good to eat, such as apples and oranges.

## fuel

Fuel is burned to make a fire, to make heat, or to make engines work. Coal, wood, oil, and gas are fuels.

## full

Full means having so much inside that there is no room for any more.

## fun

Fun means amusement. You enjoy something that is fun to do.

Something that is funny makes you laugh. Mr. Funny wears a funny hat and makes funny faces so people will laugh.

fur

## fur

Fur is thick soft hair. Most mammals have fur covering their bodies. Kittens are soft and furry.

## furious

Furious means very angry. Mr. Uppity was furious when he found that someone had scratched his brand new car.

## furniture

Furniture is all the movable things in a house. Tables, desks, chairs and beds are furniture.

## further

Further means more. Little Miss Naughty could behave herself, but she always has further mischief in mind.

Further also means a greater distance. Mr. Chatterbox walked to the garden gate. Mr. Noisy walked further. He walked across the street.

## fussy

A fussy person likes everything to be clean and neat. Mr. Fussy is so fussy, he even dusts the flowers in his garden!

## future

The future is the time that is to come. Nobody knows for certain what will happen in the future.

## gain
To gain means to get or add something to what you already have. Mr. Greedy continues to gain weight.

## gale
A gale is a strong wind.

## game
A game is an activity played with a set of rules. Football and tennis are ball games. Chess and checkers are board games. Tick tack toe and hangman are pencil and paper games.

## gap
A gap is a narrow opening. The dog ran away through a gap in the hedge.

garage

gap

## garage
A garage is a building where a car is kept.

A garage is also a place where people take their cars to be repaired or to fill them up with gas.

## garden
A garden is the land around a house or in a public place where plants are grown. Flowers, trees, and vegetables are grown in gardens.

To garden is to work in a garden. Gardening is fun.

## gas

Gas is a substance that is neither liquid nor solid. The air that we breathe is made up of several gases.

Gas is a fuel used to provide heat for stoves and furnaces. It is like air, but can be burned to give heat.

Gas or gasoline is also the liquid fuel that makes cars go.

## gasp

To gasp is to take a quick short breath.

## gate

A gate is like a door in a fence, a hedge or a wall. Gates are usually made of wood or iron.

gather

## gather

To gather means to get together. In the fall squirrels gather nuts and hide them to eat in the winter.

## gaze

To gaze at something is to stare at it because you like or admire it or because you are surprised or curious.

## generous

Generous means willing to share what you have with others.

## gentle

Gentle means kind and careful. The boy stroked the cat gently.

## geography

Geography is the study of the earth's surface and of the countries of the earth.

## get

To get something is to go for it and bring it back. Mr. Greedy went to the bakery to get some cakes.

To get to a place is to arrive there. Mr. Rush always gets home before Mr. Lazy.

To get is also to receive. Mr. Happy got lots of presents for his birthday.

## ghost

A ghost is the spirit of a dead person.

## giant

A giant is a huge strong person. You read about giants in stories.

giant

## gigantic
Gigantic means very big, like a giant.

## giggle
To giggle is to laugh in a silly way. Mr. Mischief giggled when he thought about Mr. Greedy eating pink icing that was really toothpaste.

giraffe

## giraffe
A giraffe is an animal that lives in Africa. A giraffe has a very long neck and long thin legs.

## girl
A girl is a young female person.

## give
To give means to hand something to another person. All of Mr. Silly's friends gave him Christmas presents. They were given on the Fourth of July!

To give is also to produce or to furnish something. Mr. Neat and Mr. Tidy gave Mr. Messy's house a good cleaning.

## glad
Glad means happy or pleased. Mr. Chatterbox is always glad to have someone to talk to.

## glance
To glance is to look quickly at something.

## glare
To glare is to look at someone angrily. Everyone in the library glared at Mr. Noisy when he came in talking loudly.

A glare is also a strong light.

## glass
Glass is a hard material that you can see through. Glass breaks easily. It is used for windows, bottles, and drinking glasses.

Eye glasses are worn by people to help them see better.

## globe
A globe is a round ball, usually with the map of the earth on it.

glasses

## gloomy
Gloomy means not cheerful. Nobody can be gloomy for long when Mr. Happy is around. He cheers everyone up.

gloves

### glove
Gloves are clothes you wear on your hands. Gloves fit closely and keep your hands warm. Mr. Nonsense wears blue gloves.

### glow
To glow is to shine. The lights on Christmas trees glow brightly.

glow

### glue
Glue is a substance used to stick things together. Mr. Clumsy mended his broken vase with glue, but he glued his hands together while he was gluing it!

### glum
Glum means miserable. Mr. Greedy looked glum. He had only one loaf of bread to eat for breakfast!

### gnat
A gnat is a very small flying insect.

A goat eats almost anything.

### go
To go means to move from or to a place. Mr. Greedy goes to the bakery almost every day. Yesterday he went three times! Mr. Happy saw him going home with cakes. He had already gone home with buns and bread!

To go also means to work or to act in a certain way. A gun goes off when you pull the trigger.

To go can also mean to belong. The books go on the shelf.

### goat
A goat is a mammal that has short horns and a little beard.

### goblin
goblin

A goblin is a small, man-like creature that appears in fairy tales.

## gold

Gold is a yellowish-orange metal. Rings, watches, and other jewelry are made of gold. Gold costs a lot of money.

## good

Good means not bad. Mr. Happy had a good birthday party. It was better than last year. Mr. Happy said it was the best one he ever had.

Good also means well-behaved. Mr. Mischief tried to be good and stop playing tricks on people.

## goose

A goose is a large bird. Geese have webbed feet to help them swim.

geese

## government

A government is a group of people who run a country.

## grab

To grab means to take hold of something quickly and suddenly.

## grade

A grade is a level or a place in relation to others. Most children in the first grade are six.

A grade is also a value put on something. You get grades in school.

## gradually

Gradually means little by little.

## grain

A grain is the small, hard seed of a cereal plant, or a piece of salt or sand.

## grand

Grand means large and splendid.

## grandfather

Your grandfather is the father of your mother or father.

## grandmother

Your grandmother is the mother of your father or mother.

## grass

Grass is a green plant with leaves that grow as single stalks or blades.

## grateful

Grateful means thankful to someone for doing something for you. Mr. Worry was grateful for Mr. Tall's help.

grateful

91

### gravy
Gravy is sauce made from the juices that come from meat while it is cooking.

### gray
Gray is the color of the sky on a dark, rainy day. Black and white mixed together make gray.

### graze
To graze means to scrape slightly. Mr. Bump grazed his hand on the step when he fell.

To graze also means to eat grass. The cows were grazing in the field.

### grease
Grease is an oily substance such as fat. After a breakfast of bacon and eggs, you will have a greasy plate.

Grease is also a thick oily substance used to make machines run smoothly.

### great
Great means unusually large, or important. Abraham Lincoln was a great man.

### greedy
Greedy means wanting a lot of something. Mr. Greedy's name fits him perfectly.

green

### green
Green is the color of leaves and grass. It is a mixture of blue and yellow.

greet

### greet
To greet is to welcome someone, usually with pleasure.

Greetings are friendly messages, as in Christmas greetings.

gray

### grin
To grin is to smile. You will always see Mr. Mischief grinning when he has done something naughty.

### grip
To grip is to hold something very tightly. When you climb a tree, gripping the branches firmly is important so that you do not fall.

grip

grown-up

## groan

To groan is to make a deep moaning sound because you are in pain or unhappy. Poor Mr. Lazy groaned when the bus broke down. He had to walk home!

## grocer

A grocer is a person who sells things like sugar, flour, canned foods, fruits, and vegetables in a grocery store.

## grope

To grope is to feel about with the hands. To get dressed in the dark, Mr. Busy groped for his shoes.

## ground

The ground is the surface of the earth.

The grounds of a building are the gardens and the land around the building.

Something that is ground has been cut or crushed into very small pieces, such as ground meat.

## group

A group is a number of people or things gathered together.

To group things or people is to put them together in a planned way.

## grow

To grow is to become bigger. Frank had grown so much in one year that he had to have all new clothes.

To grow flowers or vegetables is to plant them in the earth and look after them. One year Mr. Busy grew all his vegetables.

## grown-up

A grown-up is a person who is no longer a child. Parents and teachers are grown-ups. Another word for grown-up is adult.

## grumble

To grumble is to complain in a low voice. People usually grumble about things that are not very important. Mr. Grumpy always has something to grumble about, even if it is only the weather!

## grumpy

Grumpy means bad-tempered. Mr. Grumpy is always grumpy. He is rude to everyone he meets.

## grunt

To grunt is to make a deep, short sound. Pigs grunt. People sometimes grunt when they are annoyed or when they don't want to be bothered. When Mr. Happy asked Mr. Uppity the time, Mr. Uppity just grunted and walked away.

a guard on duty

## guide

To guide means to lead along or to direct. Mr. Dizzy lost his way home, so the wizard guided him back along the path.

guide

## gum

Gum is a sticky substance that comes from plants. It is used to make gum erasers. Chewing gum has a sweet flavor.

Your gums are the firm parts inside your mouth that your teeth grow from.

## gun

A gun is a weapon that fires small pieces of metal called bullets.

## gutter

A gutter is a long open area used to drain water away. There are gutters at the sides of streets. There are also gutters on a house to catch rainwater that runs off the roof.

gutter

## guard

To guard people or things is to watch over them to keep them safe. Some people keep dogs to guard their houses.

A guard is a person who watches over or protects someone or something important.

A guard is also something that prevents accidents from happening, such as bars on windows.

## guess

To guess is to say what you think is the right answer, but you are not sure. A guess may be right or wrong.

## guest

A guest is a person who visits someone else. Mr. Funny invited six guests to his birthday party.

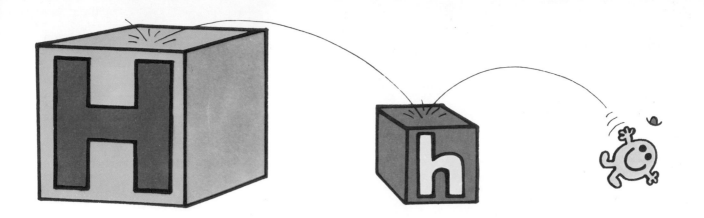

## habit

A habit is something you do without thinking because you have done it so often. It is hard to stop a bad habit, like biting your nails.

## hail

Hail is small round pieces of ice that fall from clouds in winter storms.

To hail someone is to call or greet him or her.

## hair

A hair is a very thin thread. Most people grow hair on their heads. Horses have hair all over their bodies.

## half

Half is what you get when you divide something into two parts that are the same size. Each part is a half. Two halves equal a whole.

## hall

A hall is a large room where people gather or meet.

A hall or hallway is a narrow room that connects other rooms.

hammers

Mr. Small cut the cucumber in half.

## hamburger

A hamburger is chopped beef made into a round, flat shape, then cooked and usually served on a round roll.

## hammer

A hammer is a tool with a heavy metal head that is used to hit nails into wood. Mr. Strong doesn't need a hammer. He can knock nails into the wall just by tapping them with his finger.

### hand

Your hands are at the end of your arms. Each hand has four fingers and a thumb. People hold things in their hands.

Hands are also the two pointers on a clock or watch.

To hand something means to give it with your hands.

### handkerchief

A handkerchief is a small piece of cloth you use to blow your nose in. Mr. Tall's handkerchiefs are the right size for sheets for Mr. Small's bed.

### handle

The handle of an object is the part you hold it by. Mr. Clumsy broke the handle off his teapot when he tried to pick it up.

To handle means to touch. Always handle dishes with care.

### hang

When you hang something up you fasten it at one end so that the rest of it is free. Mr. Busy is hanging his wash on the line. He hung it in the sun to dry.

hang

### happen

To happen is to take place. When Mr. Skinny heard a crashing noise he rushed to see what had happened. Mr. Clumsy had dropped some dishes again!

### happy

Happy means pleased. People smile and laugh when they are happy. Mr. Happy is nearly always happy. His happiness shows.

### harbor

A harbor is a sheltered body of water. Everyone waved as the ship sailed out of the harbor.

harbor

### hard

Hard means not easy or difficult to do. Mr. Rush finds it very hard to stay in one place for more than a minute!

Hard also means firm and solid. Butter becomes hard when it is kept in the refrigerator.

Hard can mean strong. The wind was blowing hard.

## harm

To harm is to hurt or cause damage.

## hat

A hat is a covering for the head.

## hate

To hate means to dislike very much. Mr. Messy hates taking a bath.

## have

To have something is to own it. It belongs to you. You have two arms for reaching. Mr. Tickle has extraordinarily long arms.

To have is also to feel something in a special way. Mr. Happy is having a good time, more fun than he ever had before.

To have to do something is to be required to do it. You have to eat to be healthy.

head

## hay

Hay is dried grass used as food for farm animals. Mr. Dizzy had fun sliding down a haystack when he went to the farm.

## head

Your head is the top part of your body, above your neck. It contains your brain. Your face is the front part of your head.

The head is the chief person or leader of a group.

To head a group is to lead it.

To head in a certain direction is to go that way.

## heal

To heal is to get well again. When Sarah fell off her bike she cut her knee. The cut healed quickly.

## healthy

To be healthy is to be well, to have no sickness.

## heap

A heap is a pile of things. The keeper in the park swept up the leaves and left them in a heap.

hay

### hear

To hear is to listen to sounds through your ears. Nobody can hear Mr. Quiet when he speaks because he has such a soft voice, but Mr. Noisy can always be heard.

### heart

Your heart is a very important part of your body. It keeps you alive by pumping blood through your body. If you put your hand on your chest you can feel your heart beating.

### hearty

Hearty means jolly and cheerful. Everyone laughed heartily at Mr. Funny's jokes. A hearty meal is a meal that fills you up.

### heat

Heat is hotness. It is the opposite of cold. To heat something is to make it warm or hot.

### heavy

Heavy means weighing a lot. Mr. Skinny's suitcase was heavy. Mr. Happy's was heavier. Mr. Strong's suitcase was the heaviest of all, but he could lift it easily.

### hedge

A hedge is a row of bushes or trees growing so close together that they make a wall. Hedges can be placed around the edges of fields instead of fences.

heel

### heel

Your heel is the back part of your foot.

### height

The height of something is how high or tall it is. Mr. Tall doesn't know what his height is because nobody can reach high enough to measure him!

### helicopter

A helicopter is a type of aircraft that does not have wings like an ordinary airplane. Instead, it has blades on the top that spin around very fast to keep it in the air.

helicopter

### hello

Hello is a greeting you use when you meet someone or when you answer the telephone.

## help

To help someone is to do something for someone when she or he needs you to. Little Miss Helpful wanted to help Mr. Tall, but she tied his shoelaces together instead.

## hen

A hen is a female chicken. Hens lay the eggs that we eat.

## her

Her means belonging to a female. The hat belongs to her. It is hers.

Her is also the word used when an act is done to or for a female. Mr. Forgetful bought a stamp from Mrs. Parcel. He paid her for it. She put the money away herself.

## herd

A herd is a large group of animals, especially cattle.

## here

Here means in this place.

## hesitate

To hesitate is to wait for a moment before doing something.

## hide

When you hide something you put it where nobody can see it or find it. Mr. Mischief hid Mr. Fussy's shoes. They were hidden for a week before Mr. Fussy found them.

hill

## high

Something that is high is a long way up from the ground.

## hill

A hill is a piece of ground that rises higher than the land around it.

## him

Him is the word used when something is done or given to or for a male. Mr. Forgetful bought a stamp from Mrs. Parcel. She sold it to him and he put it on the envelope himself.

## hippopotamus

A hippopotamus is a large heavy mammal that lives beside muddy rivers and pools in Africa.

## his

His means belonging to a male.

hippopotamus

hiss

## hiss
To hiss is to make a SSSSS sound. Snakes make hissing noises.

## history
History is what happened in the past.

## hit
To hit something is to touch it very hard. Tom missed hitting the ball. The ball hit the fence.

## hobby
A hobby is something you enjoy doing in your spare time. Some hobbies are stamp collecting, fishing and playing the piano.

## hold
To hold something means to keep it in your arms or hands, or to keep it inside. Mr. Fussy would not let Mr. Clumsy hold his dishes. He held them himself.

## hole
A hole is a space in or through something. Doughnuts have holes in the middle.

## holiday
A holiday is a time that marks a special occasion. On some holidays you do not work or go to school.

## home
Your home is the place where you live. Most people live in a house or an apartment.

## homework
Homework is work that teachers give students to do at home.

## honest
To be honest means to tell the truth, not to steal things or cheat.

honey

## honey
Honey is a sweet, thick liquid made by bees. You can spread honey on bread and use it in cooking.

## hop
To hop is to jump up and down on one leg. When Mr. Funny lost one of his shoes in the mud, he hopped all the way home!

## hope
To hope is to want something to happen. Mr. Small hoped that his friends would come to his party.

home

horns

## horn

Horns grow on the heads of some animals, such as bulls, rams, and deer. Horns are hard and pointed.

A horn makes a loud noise as a warning. The driver blew his horn when a child ran into the street.

Horns are also musical instruments that you blow air into to make sounds.

## horrible

Horrible means not pleasant at all. Mr. Wrong's cakes tasted horrible. He used salt instead of sugar and powder instead of flour.

## horse

A horse is a large mammal with long, strong legs. Horses are used to carry people and things. A small horse is called a pony. A baby horse is called a colt.

## hose

A hose is a long thin tube used to carry water. You use a hose to water the garden or to wash a car.

Hose is another name for socks or stockings.

## hospital

A hospital is a place where sick or injured people are cared for.

## hot

Hot means very warm. Summer mornings can be hot, but the hottest part of the day is at noon.

## hotel

A hotel is a place where people can stay when they are away from home. You pay to sleep and eat in hotels.

hotel

## hour

An hour is a length of time. An hour is 60 minutes. There are 24 hours in a day.

## house

A house is a building where people live.

## how

How means in what way. Mr. Happy told how he got to the beach. He traveled on the train.

How many means what number.

huge

## hug
To hug means to put your arms around someone and squeeze.

## huge
Huge means very big. The ship looks huge next to the tiny row boat.

## human
To be human means to be a person, not an animal. Men and women and children are humans; dogs and cats are animals.

## hungry
Hungry means wanting to eat. Mr. Greedy is always hungry.

## hunt
To hunt for something means to look for it everywhere. Mr. Messy was hunting for a pencil. His room was such a mess that he had to hunt for a long time!

## hurry
To hurry is to move as quickly as you can. Mr. Rush always hurries.

## hurt
To hurt means to be painful. Mr. Bump tripped over a large stone. His foot hurt for days afterwards.

   To hurt also means to cause pain or do harm.

## husband
A husband is the man of a married couple.

## hush
To hush is to become quiet or to tell someone else to be quiet.

## hymn
A hymn is a song about God.

### ice

Ice is frozen water. It is very slippery and cold. People skate on ice in winter. When water freezes on the streets, the streets become icy.

### ice cream

Ice cream is a cold, sweet food made from frozen cream or milk. It comes in many flavors.

### icing

Icing is a mixture made with sugar used to cover cakes.

### idea

An idea is something you think of. When his car ran out of gas, Mr. Funny had an idea. He asked Mr. Strong to carry his car to the garage. That was a good idea!

### idle

Idle means doing nothing. Mr. Lazy is idle most of the time.

Mr. Lazy is idle. He likes to sleep and not do any work.

### if

If means in case something happens. We will play outside if the sun is shining.

If also means whether. Do you know if there is candy in the jar?

### ignorant

Ignorant means knowing very little.

### ignore

To ignore someone is to pretend you haven't seen or heard him or her.

### ill

Being ill means not feeling well. People usually stay in bed when they have an illness.

### illustration

An illustration is a picture in a book or magazine. Illustrations are used in storybooks to show the reader what something in the story looks like. In this book, illustrations are used to show you what words mean.

imagine

## imagine

To imagine something is to picture it in your mind. Imagine what it would be like to live on a desert island!

## imitate

To imitate someone is to copy the way he or she speaks or acts. Mary tried to imitate the clown at the circus by making funny faces.

## immediately

Immediately means right away. The whistle was blown and the game started immediately.

## impatient

Impatient means not wanting to wait. Mr. Grumpy is very impatient. He gets annoyed if he has to wait for anything.

## important

If something is important to you, you care about it very much. Your birthday is an important day for you.

If someone or something is important, it is special or necessary. It is important to eat the right foods to be healthy.

## impossible

Something that is impossible cannot be done. Mr. Impossible jumped over a house. Nothing is an impossibility for Mr. Impossible!

## improve

To improve is to make something better or do something better than you did before.

## in

In tells the place where something is. Mr. Rush is in his house.

In can tell how or how long something is done. Mr. Rush does everything in a hurry.

## include

To include means to group together as part of a whole. Mr. Skinny's party includes Mr. Sneeze, Mr. Chatterbox, and Mr. Dizzy.

include

indeed

## increase
To increase is to grow larger or greater.

## indeed
Indeed means really. Mr. Bounce is quite small, but Mr. Small is very small indeed.

## indigestion
Indigestion is a pain people get when they have eaten too much food too quickly.

## individual
An individual is one person, a person separate from others.

## indoors
Indoors means inside a building. You have to play indoors when it is raining.

## industry
An industry is a business or group of related businesses. Many people work in the clothing industry. The U.S. is an industrial nation.

## infant
An infant is a very young baby.

## infect
To infect is to cause germs to enter a part of the body. Infections can cause pain or illness.

An infectious disease is a sickness that is passed from one person to another. Measles is infectious.

## influence
Influence is the power one person has over another that affects the way the second person acts. Mr. Neat could be a good influence on Mr. Messy.

information

## inform
To inform is to give knowledge. Information is facts. You can use books in the library to find information about many things.

## initials
A person's initials are made up of the first letter of each of his names. Roger Hargreaves' initials are R. H.

## injure
To injure means to hurt. Two people were injured in an accident. One had a broken arm and the other had a leg injury.

### insect

An insect is a small animal with six legs. Most insects have wings and can fly. Beetles, crickets and flies are all insects.

insects

### inside

Inside means in. Mr. Lazy spends most of his time inside his house sleeping!

### insist

To insist is to say something very firmly. Mr. Fussy always insists that his guests take off their shoes before they walk on his carpet.

### inspect

To inspect something means to look at it closely to see if it is all right. After Mr. Messy had washed the dishes. Mr. Fussy inspected all the plates to make sure that they were clean.

### instantly

Instantly means immediately or at once. When you push the button, the doorbell rings instantly.

### instead

Instead means in place of. Mr. Wrong wears a flowerpot on his head instead of a hat.

instead

### instruct

To instruct is to give knowledge; to teach. An instructor is a teacher.

### instrument

An instrument is an object used for a particular job. A doctor uses instruments when he or she operates on a patient.

A musical instrument is used to play music. Pianos, guitars and trumpets are all musical instruments.

instruments

## insult

To insult someone is to say something rude or hurtful to her or him.

## intelligent

Intelligent means able to understand, to think and to solve problems.

## intend

To intend to do something is to plan to do it. Mr. Slow intended to finish his book before he went to bed, but he read only two pages in three hours!

## intense

Intense means very strong. The summer sun gives off intense heat and light at noon.

## interesting

Something that is interesting makes you want to know more about it because you enjoy it. Mr. Chatterbox was watching a film that was so interesting, he actually stopped talking!

Mr. Nosey likes to interfere in matters that do not concern him.

## interfere

To interfere is to meddle with things that are not your business. When Mr. Nosey overheard two people arguing, he tried to find out what they were arguing about. Nosey people are always interfering like that!

To interfere with means to disturb or get in the way of something. The noise of the television interfered with Tom's homework. He didn't do it very well.

## interrupt

To interrupt is to break in on or to stop a person who is in the middle of something. Mr. Lazy's sleep was interrupted by Mr. Noisy who came to wake him up!

interesting

## into

Into means in, from the outside to the inside. Mr. Greedy went into the bakery.

## introduce

To introduce is to present scmeone or something to another person. Mr. Greedy introduced Mr. Skinny to the woman at the bakery.

invent

## invent

To invent means to make something for the first time. Mr. Clever invented a toaster that not only toasted bread, but spread it with butter and jelly, too. What a useful invention!

## invisible

Something that is invisible cannot be seen. It is impossible to make yourself invisible, unless you are Mr. Impossible!

## invite

To invite someone is to ask him or her to come. Mr. Forgetful invited five friends to his party. He wrote the invitations very carefully, but he forgot to mail them!

Mr. Fussy irons his clothes very carefully.

## iron

Iron is a strong gray metal. Steel is made from iron.

An iron is a heavy metal object with one flat side. You heat an iron and use it to press clothes.

## is

Is means to be or to exist. Today is Tuesday. It isn't raining now, but it was raining this morning. It has rained every day this week.

island

## island

An island is a piece of land with water all around it.

## it

It is used in place of another word or idea. Mary has a kitten. It is black and its nose is pink. The kitten washes itself.

108

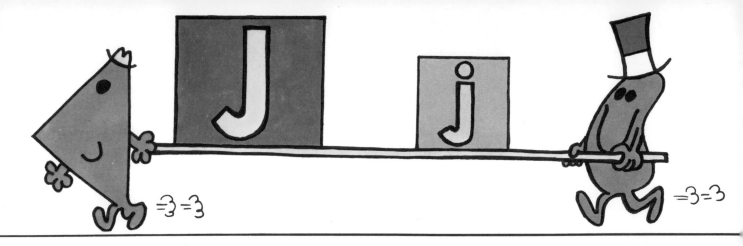

## jacket

A jacket is a short coat or a covering, such as a book jacket.

## jail

A jail is a place where people who have been convicted of a crime are locked up. Jail is also called prison.

jail

## jam

Jam is a sweet food made from boiled fruit and sugar. You spread jam on bread.

To jam means to become stuck or caught. In a traffic jam, there are so many cars on the road that none of them can move.

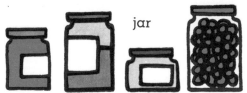

jar

## jar

A jar is a round glass container used to hold things. It has a wide opening at the top.

## jaw

Your jaws are the bones around your mouth. They hold your teeth.

## jealous

Jealous means being upset because another person has what you want. Mr. Grumpy could be jealous of Mr. Happy because Mr. Happy has so many friends.

## jeans

Jeans are pants made of thick material, usually cotton.

## jelly

Jelly is a sweet food made from fruit juice and sugar. You spread jelly on toast or bread.

## jerk

To jerk is to move suddenly and unevenly.

## jet

A jet engine is used to power a jet airplane. The plane is pushed forward by a stream of hot gas forced out behind it.

A jet is a fast-moving thin stream of liquid or gas. A jet of water shot out of the hose when the faucet was turned on.

## jewel

A jewel is a valuable stone that is used to decorate rings and necklaces. Diamonds and emeralds are jewels.

## jewelry

Necklaces, rings, bracelets and pins are all pieces of jewelry.

## jigsaw

A jigsaw is a kind of puzzle made of small pieces of shaped cardboard or wood. The pieces fit together to make a picture.

A jigsaw is a narrow saw used for cutting curves.

## jingle

To jingle is to make a ringing sound like coins or keys bumping together.

## job

A job is the work that someone does to earn a living. Mr. Quiet found a job in a library. His job was to look after the books.

## jog

To jog is to run along at a steady rate. Jogging is a popular activity.

## join

To join is to fasten two or more things together. If you break something you can sometimes join the pieces together with glue.

To join also means to become a member. Mr. Busy couldn't decide whether to join the swimming club or the sailing club, so he joined both!

## joke

A joke is something said or done that is meant to be funny. Mr. Funny loves telling jokes. Mr. Mischief plays jokes that are not always funny.

jigsaw puzzle

## jolly
Jolly means cheerful and full of fun. Mr. Happy is a jolly person. He is hardly ever angry or sad.

## journey
On a journey you travel from one place to another. Mr. Busy took three books to read on his journey to London.

## joy
Joy means happiness. Mr. Sneeze jumped for joy when he heard that the wizard could cure his cold. Mr. Sneeze was joyful.

## judge
To judge is to choose the winner in a competition. The king of Nonsenseland was the judge of the Silliest Idea of the Year contest. In his judgment, Mr. Silly was the winner.

A judge is also a person who sits in a court of law.

## jug
A jug is a container made of china, plastic or glass used to hold liquid.

## juggle
To juggle is to keep a number of objects in the air at the same time.

## juice
Juice is liquid that can be pressed out of fruits, such as oranges, by squeezing them.

## jump
To jump is to leap into the air, usually to get over something.

## jungle
A jungle is an area of land covered all over with trees, plants and bushes. Mr. Daydream landed in the jungle on one of his adventures.

## junk
Junk is anything that is considered to be trash.

## just
Just means exactly. I have just the amount of money I need.

Just is fair, right. Do you think his punishment is just?

Just also means not long ago. Guess what just happened!

## juvenile
A juvenile is a child.

jungle

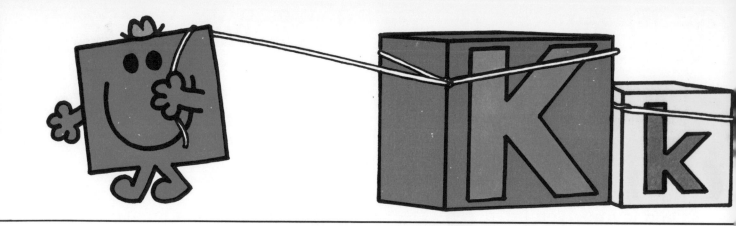

kangaroo

### kennel
A kennel is a house for many dogs.

### kettle
A kettle is a metal pot used for heating liquids. It usually has a handle and a spout.

### key
A key is a metal object that is specially shaped to lock or unlock a door. A keyhole is a hole where a key fits.

A key is also the part of a piano or other instrument that you touch with your fingers to make different sounds.

### kangaroo
A kangaroo is a large animal known as a marsupial. It has a pouch in which it carries its babies. Kangaroos have two large, strong back legs for hopping and sitting on and two very small front legs or arms.

### keep
To keep something is to have it always, not to get rid of it. Mr. Happy wanted to keep all his birthday presents.

To keep also means to have for a period of time. Mr. Clever kept the library book for two weeks.

To keep can mean to continue in the same way. Mr. Forgetful keeps forgetting to do things.

Mr. Nosey peeps through a keyhole.

## kick

To kick is to hit something or someone with your foot. Mr. Strong can kick a soccer ball over a house!

kick

## kid

A kid is a baby goat.

Kid is the leather that makes kid gloves.

A child is sometimes called a kid.

To kid someone is to tease that person.

## kidnap

To kidnap is to take a person by force and to keep him until someone pays money to set him free. When the rich man's son was kidnapped, the kidnapper refused to let the boy go until the father paid a lot of money.

## kill

To kill a person, animal or plant is to take away its life.

## kind

A kind person helps others and is friendly and gentle.

A kind also means a type or a sort. The baker sells many different kinds of cakes.

## kindergarten

A kindergarten is a class or school for young children.

## king

A king is a man who is the head of a country. The country that he is head of is called his kingdom.

## kiss

To kiss is to touch someone with your lips. Emma kisses her father and mother every night before she goes to bed.

## kit

A kit is a collection of things needed for a particular job or hobby. Mr. Bump has bandages in his first-aid kit.

kit

## kitchen

A kitchen is a room where food is cooked. Mr. Fussy's kitchen is always neat and clean.

Mr. Muddle, flying his
kite, has the string
in an awful mess!

### knack

A knack is a special ability to do
something. Mr. Happy has the
knack of cheering people up.

### knee

Your knee is the middle of your
leg, the part that bends. Mr.
Bump nearly always has bruises
and scratches on his knees.

knee

### kneel

To kneel is to bend your knees so
that one knee or both knees are
touching the floor. Mr. Clumsy
knelt down to pick up the pieces
of the plate he had dropped.

### knife

A knife is a tool used for cutting.
It has a thin sharp blade
attached to a handle. There are
lots of different kinds of knives.
There are pen-knives, kitchen
knives and table knives.

### kite

You fly a kite. It has a long
string and a wooden or metal
frame, covered with thin cloth,
paper or plastic. Wind makes
kites fly.

kitten

### kitten

A kitten is a young cat. Kittens
are small, furry and very soft.

knife

knitting

## knit

To knit is to make clothes like sweaters and scarves by looping wool between needles. Mr. Slow began knitting a pair of socks four years ago. He finished the first one yesterday!

## knob

A knob is a small round handle or switch. Doors often have knobs to open them. Mr. Clumsy pulled the knob off his radio when he tried to turn it on.

## knock

To knock is to rap with your fist or knuckles. Mr. Small knocked on the door of Mr. Quiet's house before he went in.

To knock also means to bump into or move something by accident. Mr. Clumsy knocked the cup off the shelf.

## knot

A knot is where two pieces of string or rope are tied together. You tie a knot by looping two ends around each other. When Mr. Tall's clothesline broke, he knotted the ends together.

## know

To know something is to understand it. I know how to read. I knew how to read when I was six years old. Knowing how to read well makes it easy to increase your knowledge.

To know is also to be sure. Mr. Skinny knows Mr. Greedy eats too much. Mr. Skinny has known that a long time.

knot

# L

## label
A label is a piece of paper or material that is put on something to tell about it. The label on a can of food tells what is inside it.

## labor
Labor is hard work. To labor is to work hard.

## laboratory
A laboratory is a room or building where people work to invent or study things.

## lace
Laces are long thin pieces of cotton or leather used to fasten things. Mr. Fussy irons his shoelaces to keep them neat!

Lace is also a kind of material made with a pattern of holes in it.

## ladder
A ladder is made of two long pieces of wood or metal with shorter pieces, called rungs, in between. You climb the ladder to reach something high up.

## lady
Lady is another word for woman.

## lake
A lake is an area of water with land all around it.

Mr. Bounce tried to climb the ladder, but he kept bouncing off the rungs.

## lamb

A lamb is a young sheep. Lamb is also the name of the meat we get from lambs.

## lame

To be lame means not to be able to walk well because of a problem with a leg or foot.

## lamp

A lamp is used to give light. Most lamps have electric bulbs, but some are lit by oil.

## land

Land is the dry part of the earth, the part that is not covered by water. A farmer grows crops and keeps animals on his land.

To land is to come back to the ground from the air or from water. The airplane landed safely at the airport.

## lane

A lane is a small narrow road in the country. Mr. Forgetful met some sheep in the lane.

## language

Language is made up of the words we use when we speak or write. People from different countries speak different languages. This language is English.

## lap

Your lap is the flat, top part of your legs when you are sitting down. The cat curled up on his master's lap and went to sleep.

To lap is to take up a liquid with the tongue, as a cat lapping its milk.

## large

Large means very big. An elephant is large. It is much larger than a mouse. It is the largest animal on land.

large

## larva

A larva is the young form of an insect. It hatches from an egg and looks like a small worm. A caterpillar is the larva of a butterfly.

lane

## last

Last means at the end. The last letter of the alphabet is Z.

To last means to go on for a time. You will have to make your money last all week.

Last also means the one before this. I slept well last night.

## late

Late means after the usual or proper time. When Little Miss Late worked for the bank, she was always late. By the time she arrived, the bank was closed for the day.

## laugh

To laugh is to make a sound that shows you are happy. You laugh at something that is funny. When you go to a funny play, you will hear a lot of laughter.

## laundry

A laundry is a place where clothes and sheets are washed.

To launder clothes is to wash and iron them.

Mrs. Washer is busy in the laundry washing clothes.

## lavatory

A lavatory is a room for washing your hands and face and using a toilet.

## law

A law is a rule made by a government. All the people in the country must obey the law. A lawyer is a person who studies law and gives advice.

## lawn

A lawn is the grass around your house. The grass is cut with a lawn mower to keep it short and neat.

## lay

To lay is to put down or to place something. Mr. Fussy laid his sweater carefully on the chair so that it would not get creased.

layer

## layer

A layer is one thickness of something. Mr. Greedy bought a cake that had a layer of chocolate, a layer of vanilla, and a layer of strawberry. What a cake!

## lazy
A lazy person likes to do nothing. Mr. Lazy doesn't like working. He would rather sleep all day.

## lead (It rhymes with heed.)
To lead someone is to show him or her the way. Once Mr. Wrong got lost in the woods, but Mr. Quiet led him out. The leader goes ahead of the others and acts as a guide or director. In the game "follow the leader" the players do as the leader does.

## lead (It rhymes with head.)
Lead is a very heavy gray metal. Lead is also the name for the hard black part of a pencil that makes a mark when you write with it.

## leaf
A leaf is part of a tree or plant. Leaves grow in many different shapes and sizes.

## league
A league is a group of people that have the same interests or goals, such as a baseball league.

## leak
To leak is to lose liquid or gas through a hole. Mr. Messy took a bucket of water upstairs to clean the windows, but the bucket leaked.

## leap
To leap is to jump. The horse leaped over the fence and ran across the field.

leap

## learn
To learn is to get to know about something or to find out how to do something. Children learn to read and write at school. Learning is important.

## leather
Leather is material made from the skin of a dead animal. Shoes and handbags are often made of leather.

## leave
To leave is to go away from. Mr. Happy had to leave his house early to catch a train. He left at five o'clock.

To leave also means not to take. Mr. Forgetful always leaves something behind. He left his bathing suit home when he went to the pool.

## left

The left is the opposite side to the right. When you read or write you start at the left-hand side of the page and work towards the right.

## leg

Legs are limbs for walking on. They are part of your body. You use your legs when you stand, walk, turn and jump. Mr. Tall has very long legs.

leg

## lemon

A lemon is a yellow fruit that has a very sour taste. Lemonade is a drink made with lemon juice.

lemon

## lend

To lend is to let someone use something that belongs to you for a short time. If you lend someone your pencil, you expect to get it back.

## length

The length of something is how far it is from one end to the other. You can measure the length of a line by using a ruler.

## lens

A lens is a piece of curved glass. When you look through it, a lens makes things look bigger or smaller. The glass part of a pair of eyeglasses is called a lens.

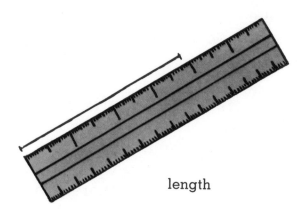

length

## leopard

A leopard is a large fierce animal of the cat family that has yellow fur with black spots.

## less

Less means a smaller amount. Mr. Skinny eats less food than Mr. Greedy.

Less also means to take away. Five less three is two.

## lesson

A lesson is something learned or to be studied. On Mondays I have music lessons.

## let

To let means to allow. My parents let me go to the circus.

To let also means to cause or make something happen.

## letter

A letter is a part of the alphabet. Letters are used to make words.

A letter is also a message that you write on paper.

## lettuce

Lettuce is a vegetable with large, green leaves. It is usually eaten raw in salads.

## liberty

Liberty is freedom, freedom to make choices.

## library

A library is a place where books are kept for people to use and to borrow. A librarian will help you find what you are looking for.

library

## lick

To lick is to move your tongue over something. She licked the ice cream until it was finished.

## lid

A lid is a cover for a container.

## lie

To lie is to stretch out flat on the floor or on a bed. The cat was lying on the rug in front of the fire.

To lie also means to say something that is not true. A person who has lied is called a liar.

## life

Your life is the time between when you are born and when you die.

## lifeboat

A lifeboat is a small open boat carried on a large ship, used to save people in danger at sea.

lifeboat

### lift
To lift something is to pick it up. Mr. Strong can lift a car with no trouble at all.

A lift is a ride, given to help someone.

### light
Light is brightness that comes from the sun, or from fire, or electric lamps. Light makes it possible for us to see. Most houses are lit with electric lights.

Light also means not heavy. A feather is very light. To lighten a load is to make it less heavy.

To light is to cause light to appear, like lighting a fire.

### lightning
Lightning is a sudden flash of light seen in the sky during a thunderstorm.

### like
To like something means to enjoy it. Mr. Chatterbox likes talking.

Like also means nearly the same as. Mr. Daydream looks like a blue cloud.

### limb
A limb is a part of your body. Legs and arms are limbs. Tree branches are also called limbs.

like

### limit
The limit is as far as you can go or as much as you can do. Drivers are not allowed to drive their cars faster than the speed limit.

### limousine
A limousine is a large expensive car. Mr. Uppity is very proud of his limousine.

### limp
To limp is to walk with some difficulty. Mr. Bump limped after he hurt his foot.

limousine

### line
A line is a long thin mark. Mr. Dizzy cannot draw a straight line, even when he uses a ruler.

A line is also a row of things or people, one behind or beside the other. There was a line of people waiting for the bus.

A line can be a rope, string, or wire. Telephone lines are wires.

To line something is to cover it on the inside. Little Miss Splendid has a coat with a fur lining.

### link
A link is something, like a ring in a chain, that connects things together

lion

## lion

A lion is a large, fierce animal that lives in the jungles of Africa and Asia. Lions are like house cats, but much bigger.

## lip

Your lips are the pink parts around your mouth. Mr. Greedy licked his lips as he sat down to his dinner.

## liquid

A liquid is anything wet that can be poured. Water and milk are liquids.

## list

A list is a number of words or names arranged one below the other. Mr. Worry made a list of all the things he had to worry about. It was a very long list indeed!

## listen

To listen is to try to hear a sound. You listen with your ears.

## literature

Literature is writing. Poems, stories, history and other printed matter are all literature.

## litter

Litter is bits of paper and other trash that are dropped on the ground. Most parks have litter baskets for people to put their trash in.

A litter is a group of baby animals born at one time.

litter

## little

Little means not big. Mr. Small is very little. He is not much bigger than a pin.

## live

To live means to be alive and not dead. Fish cannot live out of water.

To live also means to spend your time in a particular place. Mr. Funny lives in a teapot!

lizard

## lizard

A lizard is a reptile. A lizard has four short legs and a long tail.

## load

A load is something carried. Trucks carry heavy loads. To load is to put things onto something else.

## loaf

A loaf is bread cooked in one piece. Loaves have crust all around the outside.

## location

A location is the place where something is. Mr. Quiet's house is located in the middle of the woods.

Local means the area nearby.

## lock

To lock is to fasten something with a key. Mr. Nervous locks all his doors and windows at night.

## log

A log is a piece of wood from a tree. Mr. Busy likes cutting logs for his fire.

lonely

## lonely

Lonely means feeling sad because you are not with anyone. Mr. Small was lonely when he first moved into his new house. Nobody came to see him.

## long

Long means a great length from end to end. Mr. Tickle's arms are very long. He can reach all the way to the kitchen when he is lying in bed!

## look

long

To look means to use your eyes to see or find something. Everyone looked at Mr. Topsy-Turvy as he walked down the street backwards.

How something looks is the way it seems to be. Mr. Messy's house always looks messy.

## loop

A loop is a ring made by bending a piece of string or wire to cross over itself. When you tie a bow, there are two loops.

## loose

Loose means not tight. Mr. Clumsy always has loose shoelaces. To loosen something is to make it loose or looser.

Loose also means able to move easily. One of the legs on Mr. Clumsy's chair was loose.

log

## lose

To lose something is to be without it and not know where it is. Mr. Forgetful is always losing things. He thought he had lost his hat. He found it—on his head!

To lose is also to be beaten, as in a game or contest. Our team lost at baseball yesterday. It was our first loss this year.

## lot

A lot means many. Mr. Happy has a lot of friends because he is such a happy friendly person.

A lot is also a piece of land. Mr. Fussy likes things neat. Sometimes he even cleans the empty lot next door to him.

## loud

Loud means making a lot of noise or being easily heard. Mr. Noisy snores so loudly that he keeps everyone awake for miles around!

## love

To love is to like someone or something very much. Kathy loves her baby brother.

## lovely

Lovely means pleasing or pretty. Ann bought a lovely dress in the shop. She thought it was the loveliest dress she ever had.

## low

Low means not high. The tree has low branches. They are very close to the ground.

Low means soft or quiet, not loud. You whisper in a low voice.

lump

## lucky

A lucky person has good things happen to him by chance. Mr. Worry was unlucky. When he went to the beach, it started to rain. Then, luckily, the sun came out again.

## luggage

Luggage is the suitcases and bags that a person carries with him on a trip. When Mr. Forgetful went on a vacation, he left his luggage on the train!

## lump

A lump is a piece of something. The teacher gave each child a lump of clay.

A lump is also a swelling. Mr. Bump got a lump on his head when he bumped into the tree.

## lunch

Lunch is the meal that you have in the middle of the day. Some children go home for lunch. Others bring their lunches to school.

## machine

A machine is a tool with moving parts that does work for us. Some machines have motors.

## mad

Mad means very silly or crazy. Mr. Silly does mad things like putting marmalade in his coffee.
Mad also means angry.
A mad dog is sick.

## magazine

A magazine is a paper-covered book that contains stories, pictures and information. Magazines usually come out once a week or once a month.

## magic

In stories, magic is a power that witches and fairies and goblins have. Wilfred, the Wizard, gave Little Miss Bossy magic boots that made her stop being bossy. Their magic power even made her say "please."

Magic things seem unreal or impossible. A magician performs magic tricks like pulling a live rabbit out of a hat.

magic

## magnet

A magnet is a piece of metal that has the power to pull small iron objects towards it.

magnet

## magnify

To magnify something is to make it larger or to make it look larger, as with a magnifying glass.

## mail

Mail is the letters and cards and packages that are sent through the post office. To mail a letter, you put it in a mailbox or take it to the post office.

## main

Main means the most important. The main reason for going to school is to learn.

## make

To make something is to build it or put it together. Mr. Greedy made a huge sandwich for lunch.

To make also means to cause something to happen or to get someone to do something. Seeing trash in the park makes Mr. Fussy very unhappy.

To make money means to earn it. The children sold lemonade to make money.

## male

Male is the opposite of female. Men and boys are male. Bulls and roosters are male animals.

## mammal

A mammal is a warm-blooded animal. The babies of mammals are born alive. People are mammals; so are horses and dogs and cats.

## man

A man is an adult male person. Many men are fathers.

Man can also mean all human beings.

## manage

To manage is to succeed in doing something. Mr. Small managed to reach the mailbox by standing on a pile of books.

To manage is also to take charge. Mr. Greedy would like to be the manager of a bakery.

## mane

A mane is the long hair on the neck of a horse or around the head of a male lion.

## manners

Manners are a polite way of behaving. Mr. Grumpy has no manners at all. He never says "Please" or "Thank you."

## manufacture

To manufacture something is to make it by hand or by machine, usually in large amounts.

## many

Many means a large number of.

map

## map

A map is a drawing of a city or a country or the world. A map shows the shape of a country and where there are cities, rivers, lakes and mountains.

## marble

A marble is a small glass ball used in games. Most marbles have colors inside the glass.

Marble is also a kind of stone that can be polished. Statues and churches are sometimes made of marble.

## march

To march is to walk with regular steps, often in time to music.

March is also the third month.

march

## margarine

Margarine is a substitute for butter that looks and tastes nearly the same. It is made from animal or vegetable oil.

## mark

A mark is a small spot on something. When Mr. Messy has been reading a book, there are dirty marks all over the pages.

A mark is also a grade or a number that shows how well you have done on a test or a piece of school work.

## market

A market is a place where fruit and vegetables and other things are sold. Some markets are outdoors; others are in buildings. To market is to go shopping.

To market something is to have it for sale.

## marmalade

Marmalade is a thick jam usually made from oranges. Bits of peel are added to give the marmalade flavor.

## marry

When a man and a woman marry they become husband and wife. They promise that they will always love and care for each other. John and Mary were married yesterday. The marriage took place in church.

market

## marvelous

Marvelous means wonderful or very good.

## mash

To mash is to press something into a soft mass. Mr. Fussy does not like lumps in his mashed potatoes.

## mask

A mask is a covering that you wear over your face or eyes. Mr. Dizzy is wearing a mask that makes him look like a cat.

mask

## master

A master is a man who is in charge of something. The dog soon learned to obey its master.

To master something is to do it well.

## mat

A mat is a covering used to protect something. You wipe your feet on a doormat. You use placemats on the table for both decoration and protection.

## match

A match is a small stick of wood or cardboard that makes a flame when it is struck against a matchbox. Matches are not playthings.

A match is also a game played between two sides, like a tennis match.

To match is to be alike. Mr. Wrong's shoes do not match. One is black and the other is brown.

not a match

## material

Material is anything that is used to make something else. Paper is the material used to make the pages of this book.

## mathematics

Mathematics is the science of numbers, measurements and amounts.

## matter

To matter is to be important. Mr. Clumsy broke one of Mr. Happy's cups. Mr. Happy said it didn't matter; it was already chipped.

Matter also means substance.

## mattress

A mattress is the large, thick pad on a bed.

## may

May means possible. It may rain tomorrow. Maybe it will rain.

May also means permission. Mother said I may play outside.

May is the fifth month.

## maze

A maze is a sort of puzzle. A maze has many paths so that it is difficult to find your way out.

a maze of hedges

## me

Me is a form of I. "I have a green hat," said Mr. Chatterbox. "The hat belongs to me. It is mine."

## meadow

A meadow is a field of grass.

## meal

A meal is the food that you eat at certain times. Breakfast is the first meal of the day.

## mean

What a word means is what it stands for. Small means not big.

To mean to do something is to do it on purpose. Mr. Clumsy did not mean to break the teapot; it slipped out of his hand. He meant to put it away.

Mean also means selfish and not kind to others.

## measles

Measles is a disease. When you have measles your body has red spots all over it and you feel ill.

## measure

To measure is to find the size of something.

## meat

Meat is the flesh of an animal, which is used as food. Pork is meat that comes from a pig.

## medal

A medal is a piece of metal like a coin that is given to someone as a prize, or because he has done something outstanding or brave. Our team won two gold medals and one silver medal in the swimming contest.

## medicine

Medicine is a liquid or pill that the doctor gives you when you are ill. You take the medicine to help you get better.

## meet

To meet is to come together with someone. You may meet a person by chance, or you may plan to meet at a particular time. Mr. Happy met Mr. Greedy in the candy store.

A meeting happens when a group of people get together for a special reason. Cub Scouts hold meetings once a week after school.

meet

## melt

To melt is to change something from solid to liquid by heating it. Mr. Silly built a snowman in his kitchen! It melted and left a puddle of water on the floor.

melt

## member

A member is someone who belongs to something like a club, a group or a church. Only members of the swimming club are allowed to use the pool.

## memory

Your memory is the part of your brain that helps you to remember things. Mr. Forgetful has a very bad memory. Sometimes he cannot even remember his name!

## menace

A menace is someone or something that could cause trouble or danger. Little Miss Helpful tried to be nice, but when she was helpful she was really a menace!

## mend

To mend something is to put it together again after it has been broken or torn.

## mental

Mental means having to do with the mind.

## mention

To mention is to speak about. When I talked to Kate's father, he mentioned that she had gone to school early.

## menu

A menu is a list of the food that you can choose from in a restaurant.

## mermaid

A mermaid is a make-believe creature, half woman and half fish, who lives in the sea.

mermaid

## merry

Merry means jolly and full of fun. Mr. Busy whistled a merry tune as he did his housework.

## mess

A mess is an untidy or dirty group of things; a confused heap.

## message

A message is a few words sent from one person to another. Mother sent a message to the teacher to say that Amy was sick and could not go to school.

## messenger

A messenger is a person who delivers a message. Mr. Forgetful is not a good messenger, because he can never remember the message he is supposed to deliver!

messenger

## messy

Messy means untidy or dirty, not neat. Mr. Messy never puts things away, or cleans his house, or weeds his garden. He is a messy person!

## metal

Metal is a solid such as iron or silver. Many metals have shiny surfaces when they are polished. Metal is used to make things like engines and machines and cans.

## microphone

A microphone is used to make sounds louder or to direct sounds in a certain way.

## microscope

A microscope is used to see very small things or things that cannot be seen with the eye alone. It has lenses in it that make things look bigger.

microscope

## middle

The middle of something is its center. It is the same distance away from all the sides. There are white lines down the middle of most main roads.

## midnight

Midnight is 12 o'clock at night.

## might

Might means power. He threw the ball with all his might.

Might means possibly. Mr. Grumpy might learn to smile.

## milk

Milk is a liquid food. We drink milk that comes from cows. Milk comes from female animals.

## mill

A mill is a factory where things are made. Wheat is milled into flour at a flour mill.

## mind

Your mind is the part of your brain that you use to think and learn and remember. To change your mind means to decide to do something different.

To mind is to be upset or to care about something. Mr. Lazy didn't mind that Mr. Slow was an hour late. It meant he could sleep for an hour longer!

To mind also means to look after. The baker asked his assistant to mind the store while he baked more bread.

To mind is also to obey. You should always mind your parents.

## mine

Mine means belonging to me. That book is mine.

A mine is a place underground where miners work to dig up minerals.

## mineral

A mineral is a substance that is formed by nature in the ground. Coal, salt and gold are minerals.

## mint

A mint is the place where money is made or stamps are printed.

Mint is a plant used for flavoring.

## minus

Minus means less. Five minus two is three.

## minute

A minute is a length of time. There are 60 seconds in a minute. There are 60 minutes in an hour.

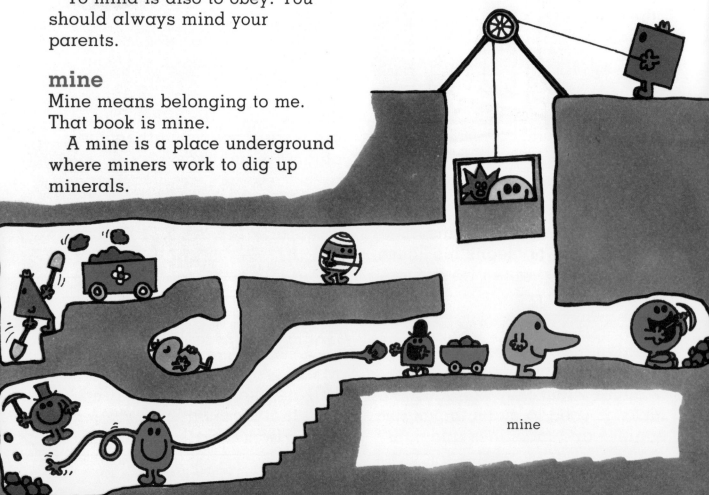

mine

mirror

### miracle

A miracle is an extraordinary happening that is beyond what is usually possible. It would be a miracle if you could hear Mr. Quiet over Mr. Chatterbox or Mr. Noisy.

### mirror

A mirror is a piece of glass with a silver backing. You can see yourself in a mirror. Mr. Funny looked in the mirror and saw that he had his hat on upside down!

### mischief

Mischief means bad or annoying behavior. To be mischievous is to play tricks on people like Mr. Mischief always does.

### miserable

Miserable means not happy or not cheerful. Mr. Dizzy is often miserable because everyone laughs at the silly things he says.

### miss

To miss is not to hit or catch something. Mr. Clever threw the ball to Mr. Clumsy, but Mr. Clumsy missed it.

To miss also means to notice that someone is away or that something is not there. Jennifer missed her mother while she was staying with her grandmother. Mr. Stingy counts his money to be sure none is missing.

A miss is a young woman or girl. Little Miss Sunshine makes people smile.

### mistake

A mistake is something that is wrong. Mr. Wrong worked as a waiter in a restaurant, but he had to leave because he made so many mistakes.

### mitten

A mitten is a covering for your hand. It has a place for your thumb and another place for the rest of your fingers.

mistake

## mix

To mix is to put several things together. You mix flour and water together to make paste.

To mix up means to muddle or confuse. Mr. Muddle is always getting things mixed up. For instance, he will say, "Good morning," when he should be saying, "Good night!"

## moan

To moan is to complain. Mr. Grumpy moaned when Mr. Happy left the door open and let cold air into the room.

To moan also means to make a low crying sound because you are in pain or unhappy.

## model

A model is a small exact copy of a larger object. Michael made a model airplane from a kit.

A model is also a person who wears new clothes to show to other people.

model

## modern

Modern means of the present time. My grandfather does not like modern inventions. He would rather ride in a horse drawn wagon than a spaceship.

## modest

A modest person does not boast about himself or show off. Susan is modest. She did not tell her uncle she is the best swimmer in the class.

## mole

A mole is a small mammal with dark velvety fur and a long nose. Moles are a nuisance to gardeners because they make molehills in the lawn and destroy plants.

mole

## moment

A moment is a very short space of time. You can blink your eyes in a moment. It takes only a moment to say "Hello."

## money

Money is the coins and bills we use to buy things and to pay people. Mr. Uppity has lots of money. He is the richest person in Bigtown.

monkey

## monkey

A monkey is a mammal that has hands and feet like a human being. Monkeys are covered with hair and have long tails. Monkeys are very intelligent and can do tricks.

## monocle

A monocle is a glass lens that is worn over just one eye. A monocle helps you to see better. Mr. Uppity wears a monocle.

monocle

## monster

A monster is a large, frightening creature. Monsters usually appear in horror stories, but they do not really exist.

monster

## month

A month is a length of time. There are 12 months in a year, and each one has a different name. All the months except February have 30 or 31 days.

## mood

A mood is the way that you feel at a particular time. Mr. Happy is nearly always in a good mood.

## moon

The moon is a satellite of the earth. It moves around the earth and shines in the sky at night.

## mop

A mop is a piece of equipment used to clean or polish floors. It has a long handle with a head of soft material at one end.

mop

## more

More means a larger amount. Mr. Happy eats more food than Mr. Skinny. Mr. Greedy eats the most.

More also means other. Mr. Fussy wished that Mr. Mischief would not do any more tricks.

137

## morning

The morning is the first half of the day. Morning is the time between midnight and midday.

moth

## most

Most means the biggest amount, or more than anything else.

## moth

A moth is an insect that usually flies at night. A moth is like a butterfly, but its wings are not as brightly colored.

## mother

A mother is a woman who has a child.

## motor

A motor makes a machine work. The motor of a car is what makes it go. A motorboat is a boat that is driven by a motor.

mountain

## mountain

A mountain is a piece of land that rises up much higher than the land around it. A mountain is higher than a hill.

## mouse

A mouse is a small furry animal with a long tail. Some mice live in houses and others in fields.

moustache

## moustache

A moustache is the hair that grows on the upper lip. Mr. Slow has a white moustache.

## mouth

You open and close your mouth to eat, drink and talk.

## move

To move is to put something in a different place. Mr. Happy moved all his furniture so that he could paint the walls.

To move is also not to stay still. Mr. Busy is always moving around, doing something.

To move also means to start to live in a different place, with a new address.

## mow

To mow is to cut, as grass or hay. Mr. Busy mows his lawn every day.

## much

Much means a large amount. It rained so much today that there are deep puddles everywhere.

## mud

Mud is soft wet earth. Mr. Messy was covered with mud after his walk in the country. He was a muddy mess!

## muddle

To muddle is to mix things up by mistake. Mr. Muddle sometimes wears his shoes on his hands and his gloves on his feet!

## mug

A mug is a large cup that is used without a saucer. Mr. Sneeze has a mug with his name on it.

## mumble

To mumble is not to speak clearly.

## multiply

To multiply is to add the same number together a number of times. When you multiply three times two, the answer is six.

To multiply is also to grow in number. The weeds in Mr. Messy's garden multiplied every year, because he never pulled them out.

## mumps

Mumps is a disease that you catch from someone. When you have mumps the sides of your face become swollen and sore.

muscle

mug

## murder

Murder is killing someone.

## muscle

Your muscles are part of your body. Muscles help you to move and lift and hold things.

museum

## museum

A museum is a building where interesting things are displayed and studied.

## mushroom

A mushroom is a plant usually shaped like a small umbrella. You can eat some kinds of mushrooms, but others are poisonous.

mushrooms

## music

Music is the sound made by musical instruments and by people when they sing.

Music is also the written notes for a particular piece of music.

A musician is a person who plays a musical instrument.

music

## must

If you must do something, you are forced or required to do it. You must buy a ticket to ride on the train.

## mustard

Mustard is a yellow powder or liquid made from the seeds of the mustard plant. It has a strong taste

## mutter

To mutter is to speak in a low voice, as if you don't want people to hear. Mr. Stingy muttered about the price of food when he went shopping.

## my

My means belonging to me. Myself is another word for me. I burned myself.

## mystery

A mystery is a strange thing or a secret that we cannot easily understand or explain. How Mr. Impossible becomes invisible is a mystery.

nail

## nail

A nail is a thin round piece of metal with a sharp point at one end. Nails are hammered into pieces of wood to hold them together.

A nail is also the hard covering at the end of a finger or toe.

## name

The name of a person or place is the word he or it is known by.

## nap

A nap is a short sleep. Mr. Lazy likes to have a nap after lunch.

## napkin

A napkin is a piece of cloth or paper that we use to keep our hands, face and clothes clean when we eat.

nap

## narrow

Narrow means not wide. Mr. Greedy tried to squeeze through a narrow opening in the fence, but he got stuck, because he was too wide.

narrow

## nation

A nation is the people of one country under one rule. The United States is a large nation.

## natural

Natural means made by nature, not by people. Honey is a natural food. Some people have naturally curly hair.

## nature

Nature is the universe and everything that is in it that has not been made by people. Nature is also the way things are and usually act, like human nature.

## naughty

Naughty means behaving badly. When Little Miss Naughty tripped Mr. Busy, she was very naughty.

## navy

The navy is all the warships that belong to a country and all the sailors who serve on them.

Navy blue is a very dark blue color.

These three ships and their sailors are all part of one navy.

## near

Near means not far away. There is a park near our house where we play. It takes only five minutes to walk there.

## nearly

Nearly means almost. Robert is nearly nine years old. His birthday is next month.

## neat

Neat means tidy. Mr. Fussy writes very carefully and neatly. It is easy to read his writing.

## necessary

If something is necessary it is something that you must do or have. It is necessary to buy a ticket in order to travel on the train.

neck

## neck

Your neck is the part of your body that joins your head to the top of your shoulders. Mr. Snow wears a scarf around his neck.

A necklace is jewelry that you wear around your neck, like beads or a chain.

## need

If you need something you must have it. You need money to shop.

needle

## needle

A needle is a thin piece of metal with a hole in it for thread. It is used for sewing.

## neglect

To neglect means not to care for or look after. Mr. Messy neglects his house. It looks neglected.

neglect

## neighbor

A neighbor is a person who lives next door to or near you. Mr. Nosey always likes to know what his neighbors are doing. Sometimes he peeps through their windows to find out!

## neighborhood

A neighborhood is an area of a town or city. There are good schools in our neighborhood.

## neither (and nor)

Neither means not one or the other. Neither Mr. Happy nor Mr. Worry wears a hat. (Nor means "not or" and is only used with neither.)

neither

## nervous

Nervous means worried about something that is going to happen. Tim is always very nervous before a test at school. He is afraid that he might not know the answers.

nest

### nest

A nest is a bird's home. Many birds build their nests out of twigs and grass and mud.

### net

A net is a piece of loosely made material that has even rows of holes in it. You can catch butterflies or fish in nets.

### never

Never means not at any time. Mr. Greedy can never get enough to eat.

### new

New means not old or used. Peter bought a new pair of shoes. His old ones were worn out.

### news

News is information about things that have just happened. Mr. Clever listens to the news on the radio every morning.

A newspaper is several printed sheets of paper folded together. Newspapers give information about news, sports and other things that have happened or will happen soon.

### next

Next means after this. Mr. Tickle has just tickled the postman. Next he is going to tickle the policeman.

Next to means alongside. The bakery is next to the supermarket.

next

### nibble

To nibble is to eat something by biting off a small piece at a time. The rabbit nibbled a lettuce leaf. leaf.

### nice

Nice means pleasant or pleasing. Mr. Happy had a nice time at the beach.

### nickel

A nickel is a coin that is worth five pennies.

## nickname

A nickname is a name your friends use instead of your real name. Claire's name is "Red," because she has red hair.

## night

Night is the time between sunset and dawn when the sky is dark.

nightmare

## nightmare

A nightmare is a very bad dream. Mr. Nervous had a nightmare about being chased a lion.

## no

No is the opposite of yes. You are told no when you cannot have or do something you want.

No also means not any. Mr. Skinny eats no candy.

Nobody means no person. Nowhere means no place.

## nod

To nod is to move your head down and up. Mr. Quiet nodded his head to say yes.

## noisy

Something that is noisy makes a lot of noise so you can easily hear it. Mr. Noisy sneezes so loudly that you can hear him all over town.

## none

None means not any. Mr. Greedy has four cakes on his plate but Mr. Skinny has none.

## nonsense

Nonsense is something silly that is not true. Mr. Nonsense says that dogs wear hats and sheep can fly. What nonsense!

## noon

Noon is 12 o'clock in the daytime. We eat lunch at noon.

## normal

Normal means usual, the same as others. It is normally cold in winter.

### north

North is the direction toward the top of the earth. The North Pole is the northern part of the earth.

### nose

Your nose sticks out in the middle of your face. You breathe and smell through your nose.

### not

Not means the same as no, the opposite of yes. Mr. Grumpy does not like to smile.

### note

A note is a short, written message.

A note is also a sound in music.

### nothing

Nothing means no thing, not anything.

### notice

A notice is a written message. It is put in a place where everyone can read it.

To notice something is to see it. Mr. Robinson noticed Mr. Small just in time!

notice

### now

Now means at this time. The sun is shining now.

### nuisance

A nuisance is a person or thing that annoys you.

### number

A number is a symbol or word that you count with. A number tells how many.

### nurse

A nurse is someone who helps the doctor take care of sick people.

### nursery

A nursery is a place where very young children are cared for.

A nursery is also a place where plants are grown.

nurse

### nut

A nut is the fruit or seed of certain trees. It usually has a hard outside shell. You can eat the soft inside of many nuts, such as peanuts and walnuts.

nuts

oar

To object to something is not to like it or not to approve of it. Mother objected when Mary wanted to watch television until midnight.

## oar
an oar is a long, wooden pole with a wide, flat end. Two oars are used to row a row boat.

## obey
To obey someone is to do what he or she tells you. Sally obeyed her mother and came home right after school. Sally was obedient.

## object
An object is a thing that you can see and touch. A ball is a round object.

The object of doing something is the purpose or reason for doing it. The object of baseball is to score runs.

oblong

## oblong
An oblong is a shape with four sides. Two opposite sides of the shape are longer than the other two.

## observe
To observe is to look at something carefully.

## obstacle
An obstacle is something that gets in the way. The bus had to stop because there was an obstacle in its way.

object

### obvious

Something that is obvious is easy to see or understand. There is obviously something wrong with my watch. It keeps stopping.

### occasionally

Occasionally means once in a while. Mr. Chatterbox occasionally stops talking.

### occur

To occur is to happen. The accident occurred at lunch time.

When something occurs to you, it means you suddenly think of it.

### ocean

An ocean is a great area of water that surrounds land.

### o'clock

O'clock means time shown by the clock. It is one o'clock.

### octopus

An octopus is an animal that lives in the sea. It has eight long arms called tentacles.

odd

### odd

Odd means strange. Mr. Silly built an odd car. It had square wheels!

Odd also means not matching. Mr. Wrong wears odd gloves and shoes.

An odd number is not even. If you divide an odd number by two, there will always be one left over. Three, seven and 11 are odd numbers.

### odor

An odor is a smell.

### of

Of means belonging to. Mr. Clumsy broke one of Mr. Happy's cups.

Of also means from. Some houses are made of wood.

Of can also mean what material is in something, as in a glass of milk.

### off

Off means not on. The radio is off, means that it is not working.

Off also means away from.

octopus

## offer

To offer something is to ask someone if he wants it. Mr. Happy offered his guest a drink.

To offer also means to say you are willing to do something. Mr. Neat offered to clean Mr. Messy's house.

## office

An office is a room or a building where people work, like a doctor's office.

To hold office is to have a special or important job. A general is an army officer.

oil

## often

Often means many times. Mr. Lazy often falls asleep watching television.

## oil

Oil is a thick greasy liquid.

To oil is to put oil on or in something to make it work better.

## old

Old shows age. Old is the opposite of young or new. David is five-years-old. He got new shoes and gave away his old ones.

## on

On tells where something or someone is. Alison is on the floor.

On means not off. The radio is on. It is working.

On can show time. Jessica went swimming on Saturday.

## once

Once means one time. Mr. Grumpy went to the circus once.

Once also means right now. Come here at once!

Once can mean at the same time. We all laughed at once.

open

## one

One means a single person or thing. One is also the number 1.

## only

Only means no more than. There are only four cookies in the jar.

## open

Open means not shut. Mr. Fussy opened his window to let fresh air into the room.

## operate

To operate something is to make it run or work.

opposite

## opinion
Your opinion is what you think or believe about something.

## opposite
The opposite means the most different. Hot is the opposite of cold. Yes is the opposite of no.

Opposite also means on the other side.

orange

## or
Or shows a choice between two things.

## orange
Orange is the color made from red and yellow.

An orange is a round, juicy fruit with thick, orange skin.

## orbit
An orbit is the path that one object takes as it moves around another in space.

## orchard
An orchard is a piece of land where fruit trees are grown.

## orchestra
An orchestra is a large group of people who play musical instruments together.

## order
The order is the way that things are arranged. The entries in this dictionary are in alphabetical order, the same order as the letters in the alphabet.

An order is also something you must obey. Soldiers are trained to obey orders from their officers.

## ordinary
Ordinary means usual or common. Mr. Happy lives in an ordinary house, but Mr. Clever's house is not ordinary at all. In fact, it's extraordinary!

## organ
An organ is a musical instrument.

An organ is also a part of your body. Your heart and liver are organs.

## organize
To organize is to arrange something or put it in order.

not an
ordinary
house

## original

Something that is original has not been done or thought of before. Mr. Silly's original idea won the Nonsense Cup.

## ornament

An ornament is something that decorates. Mr. Fussy puts his Christmas tree ornaments away carefully every year.

## orphan

An orphan is a child whose parents are not living.

original

## ostrich

An ostrich is a bird with a long neck and long legs. Ostriches have wings, but they cannot fly.

## other

Other means different, remaining or opposite.

ostrich

## ought

Ought means should. Mr. Messy ought to clean his house.

## our

Our means that something belongs to us. This is our house.

## out

Out means away from the inside, or not in.

Out also means off. The lights are out.

## outfit

An outfit is a set of clothes that you wear together. James got a cowboy outfit for his birthday.

## outline

The outline of anything is the line around its outside edge. Mr. Clever has drawn an outline of his hand.

To outline something is to show the main parts of it.

outline

## outside

Outside means not inside. Mr. Lazy likes to lie outside on a sunny day, sleeping in the sun.

## oval

Oval means egg-shaped. Mr. Forgetful has an oval body, but Mr. Worry has a round body.

oval

## oven

An oven is the part of a stove where you put food to bake or roast. It is a heated box with a door.

## over

Over means ended. School is over at three o'clock.

Over means across, to the other side. Josh jumped over the fence.

Over also means above. A bird flew over the house.

Over can mean again. Mr. Chatterbox says the same thing over and over!

Over can also mean down. Mr. Rush was in such a hurry, he almost knocked Mr. Quiet over.

Over means more than. I have over five dollars in the bank.

## overflow

To overflow is to spill over the top of something because too much has been put in. Mr. Forgetful's bath overflowed, because he forgot to turn the water off.

## overhear

To overhear is to hear something that you are not meant to hear.

## owe

To owe is to be in debt and to have to pay back someone for something. Mr. Slow owes the library money for not returning his books on time.

## owl

An owl is a night bird with a large head and eyes.

owl

## own

To own something is to have it belong to you.

Something that is your own is yours and doesn't belong to anyone else. Pat uses her own pen at school.

## ox

An ox is a large animal used for work. Oxen are used on farms.

## pack

To pack is to put things into a box, bag or case. Mr. Happy packed his suitcase before he took a trip.

A pack is a group of things together, such as a pack of gum.

## package

A package is a box or container that is wrapped.

## pad

A pad is a lot of sheets of paper stuck together at one edge. Robert wrote the telephone message on a pad so he wouldn't forget it.

A pad is also thick material used to make something more comfortable or for protection. Football players wear pads to protect themselves.

## paddle

A paddle is a kind of oar. It has a short, wooden handle and a flat end for pushing a canoe through water.

To paddle is to splash around in the water with your hands or feet.

## page

A page is a sheet of paper in a book or a magazine or a newspaper. Mr. Grumpy tears the pages out of his books when he gets upset.

## pail

A pail is a container of metal, wood or plastic with a handle.

pages

## pain

Pain is an unpleasant feeling. You feel pain when you are hurt. Mr. Wrong had a pain in his foot, so he went to the dentist!

pad

153

paint

## paint

Paint is a liquid that is used to color things. Mr. Messy painted his front door with orange paint.

## painting

A painting is a picture or design that is made with paints.

## pair

A pair is two things that match, such as a pair of gloves or a pair of shoes.

Sometimes a pair is one object that has two matching parts. A pair of pants has two legs, and a pair of scissors has two blades.

## pajamas

Pajamas are nightclothes, a kind of suit to sleep in.

## palace

A palace is a large, grand building. Kings and queens live in palaces.

## pale

Pale means light in color. People's faces often become pale when they are ill or when they are frightened.

## palm

The palm of your hand is the flat part on the inside. Mr. Small is so tiny you could hold him in the palm of your hand.

A palm is also a tall tree found in hot places. Dates and coconuts grow on different kinds of palm trees.

palm

## pamper

To pamper someone is to treat that person almost too well.

## pan

A pan is a pot for cooking. Most pans have a handle and a lid. Frying pans are not very deep and are used to fry food. Saucepans are used on top of the stove for boiling and stewing food.

## pancake

A pancake is a food made from flour, eggs and milk. Pancakes are round and thin and are often cooked in a frying pan.

panda

## panda

A panda is an animal that looks like a bear. It lives in China and has white fur with black patches on its legs and ears and around its eyes.

## pane

A pane is a piece of glass in a window.

## panic

To panic is to be suddenly frightened and not know what to do. Mr. Nervous panicked when he saw a scarecrow. He thought it was a monster.

## pant

To pant is to breathe in short gasps. You pant when you have been running very fast.

## pants

A pair of pants is a piece of clothing worn around the waist and on the legs.

## paper

Paper is a thin material that you write on. The pages in this book are made of paper.

## parachute

A parachute is used to jump from a flying airplane. The parachute helps you float safely down to the ground.

## parade

A parade is a group of people marching together. There are musicians, animals, and clowns in circus parades.

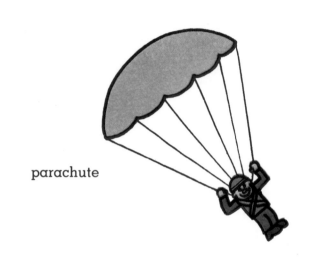
parachute

## parcel

A parcel is a package or a bundle.

## pardon

To pardon is to forgive someone for doing something wrong or unpleasant.

## parent

A parent is a father or a mother.

## park

A park is a piece of land in a town where people go to enjoy themselves.

To park a car is to leave it in a place by the side of a road or in a parking lot.

parrot

## parrot

A parrot is a bird with brightly colored feathers. Some people keep parrots as pets. Parrots can be taught to talk.

## particular

Particular means only this one and not any other. At this particular moment, you are reading the Mr. Men™ and Little Miss™ Picture Dictionary.

To be particular means to be especially careful. Mr. Fussy is particular about everything; he wants everything exactly right.

partners

## partner

A partner is a person who joins with you to do something. Mr. Busy chose Mr. Rush for his partner in a three-legged race.

## party

A party is a time when people come together to enjoy themselves. On his birthday, Mr. Happy had a party for all his friends.

## pass

To pass means to go by. Time passes. When he passes a house, Mr. Nosey always peeps through the window to see what is going on.

To pass something also means to hand or move it from one person or place to another. Mr. Silly asked Mr. Nonsense to pass him a blue orange.

To pass a law is to make a rule that must be obeyed.

## passage

A passage is a narrow path or tunnel. The robbers escaped through a secret passage in the castle.

Passage is also moving from one time or one place to another.

passage

passengers

## passenger
A passenger is a person who travels in a vehicle that someone else is driving. There are six passengers on the bus.

## past
The past is time that is over or finished. In years past, there were no airplanes or spaceships.

Past also means beyond a place. Mr. Uppity walked right past Mr. Happy without saying "Hello."

## paste
Paste is a thick mixture used to stick things together.

## pastry
Pastry is a mixture of flour, fat or oil and water. Pastry is used to make pies and other sweets.

## pasture
A pasture is a grassy field where cattle and horses graze.

## pat
To pat is to hit or touch lightly.

## patch
To patch something is to repair it or put it back together.

A patch is a small piece of material used to cover a hole or a worn place.

## path
A path is a narrow road where people can walk through the woods, or in a garden, or by a river.

## patient
A patient person is content to wait calmly for something and not complain. Mr. Slow is very patient. He waited two hours for the bus to arrive, and he wasn't upset at all.

A patient is a sick person who is being taken care of by doctors and nurses.

## pattern
A pattern is a design made up of colors, shapes or lines arranged in a particular way. Wallpaper and dress materials are often decorated with patterns.

pattern

**pause**
To pause is to stop for a minute.

**pavement**
A pavement is the walkway along the side of a road. A pavement is usually made of hard material like concrete.

**paw**
A paw is the foot of an animal.

**pay**
To pay is to give money for something being bought or for work done. Mr. Topsy-Turvy paid the taxi driver.

To pay a visit to someone is to go to that person's house.

pay

**pea**
A pea is a vegetable that is the round, green seed of a plant. Peas grow together inside a pod.

**peace**
Peace is a time when there is no war.

Peace also means quiet and stillness. Mr. Quiet likes to live in the peaceful countryside. He can sleep peacefully there.

peach

**peach**
A peach is a soft, juicy fruit with a furry skin. Peaches grow on trees.

pear

**peanut**
A peanut is a kind of bean that looks and tastes like a nut.

**pear**
A pear is a green or yellow fruit that grows on a tree and is shaped like a bell.

**pebble**
A pebble is a small, round, smooth stone.

**peculiar**
Peculiar means strange or unusual. Mr. Funny lives in a peculiar place, a teapot!

**pedal**
A pedal is a part of a machine that is worked by foot. When you ride a bicycle, you put your feet on two pedals to make the wheels go around. Cars, sewing machines, and pianos also have pedals.

pedal

**peel**
To peel is to take the outer skin off a fruit or vegetable.

## peep
To peep is to take a quick look at something. Mr. Nosey peeped through the fence to see what was on the other side.

## pen
You use a pen to write with ink. There are felt-tip pens, fountain pens and ballpoint pens.

A pen is also a place to keep animals.

## pencil
A pencil is used for writing and drawing. It has lead in the middle.

## penguin
A penguin is a bird that cannot fly. Penguins have white fronts, with black or gray backs and tails.

penguin

## penny
A penny is a piece of money, a coin that is one cent. Five pennies make a nickel.

## people
People means a number of men, women or children. There wre a lot of people on the beach, because it was such a hot day.

## pepper
Pepper is a powder that you put on food to give it flavor. Pepper can be black, white, red or green and has a hot taste. Some fresh peppers taste sweet.

## perfect
Something that is perfect has nothing wrong with it at all. Mr. Fussy is very proud of his perfect lawn. Every blade of grass is neatly cut and perfectly straight.

## perform
To perform is to entertain people in a theater or a hall. The children performed a play at the end of the school year.

perform

## perhaps
Perhaps means maybe. Perhaps it will rain tomorrow.

## period
A period is a length of time. We went camping for a period of two weeks.

A period is also the dot at the end of a sentence.

## permanent
Something that is permanent is always there and does not change much. The smile on Little Miss Sunshine's face is permanent, because she is always happy.

## permit
To permit is to allow someone to do something. You are permitted to fish in the river if you ask.

permit

## perplexed
Perplexed means puzzled or confused. Mr. Clever was perplexed when Mr. Small asked how he could grow bigger. Mr. Clever didn't know.

## person
A person is a man or woman or child. Everyone is a person.

## persuade
To persuade is to convince someone to do something. Mr. Happy persuaded Mr. Miserable to smile.

## pest
A pest is someone or something that is a nuisance. Some insects are pests because they kill plants. Mr. Mischief is sometimes a pest.

pet

## pet
A pet is an animal that lives with people and is taken care of by them. People keep dogs and cats as pets.

## petal
A petal is one of the colored parts of a flower. Daffodils have yellow or white petals.

## petroleum
Petroleum is a liquid fuel that comes from oil. It is used to make engines work. Cars and motorcycles use petroleum in the form of gasoline.

## phonograph

A phonograph is a machine that plays records to make sounds. It is also called a record player.

## photograph

A photograph is a picture taken with a still camera.

## piano

A piano is a large musical instrument that has a row of

piano

white and black keys. Mr. Noisy is the pianist.

## pick

To pick is to choose. Mr. Greedy always picks the biggest cakes when he goes shopping.

To pick also means to gather something that is growing. You pick apples in the fall.

To pick up means to lift. Mr. Strong picked up a heavy stone with no effort at all.

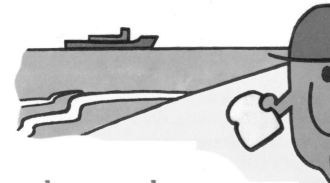

picnic

## picnic

A picnic is a meal that you eat outside. Mr. Clumsy and Mr. Muddle had a picnic at the beach. Mr. Clumsy dropped his sandwich in the sand!

## picture

A picture is a drawing or a painting or a photograph. Mr. Messy likes painting pictures, but he always gets paint all over the floor and himself.

## pie

A pie is pastry filled with fruit or meat or some other kind of food. Pies are baked in the oven.

## piece

A piece is a part that is broken off or cut away from something. Mr. Muddle gave Mr. Clumsy a piece of his bread.

## pierce

To pierce something is to make a hole in it, usually with something sharp.

pig

## pig

A pig is an animal that lives on a farm. It has a flat snout for a nose and a short, curly tail. Pork, ham and bacon come from pigs.

## pile

A pile is a heap of things, one on top of the other. Mr. Messy always has piles of dirty dishes in his kitchen.

## pill

A pill is a small piece of medicine. Sometimes the doctor gives you pills to take when you are ill.

## pillow

A pillow is a soft pad that you rest your head on in bed. It is made from a cloth bag filled with something soft and light like feathers or foam.

## pilot

A pilot is a person who flies an airplane.

pilot

## pin

A pin is a small thin piece of metal with a sharp point at one end and a round or flat head at the other. Pins are used to hold pieces of material or paper together. Mr. Clever is very good at pinning things.

## pinch

To pinch is to nip or squeeze something between your finger and thumb. Allan cried when his sister pinched his arm.

## pink

Pink is a color made by mixing red and white together. Little Miss Helpful is pink.

pink

## pipe

A pipe is a hollow tube made of metal, plastic or rubber. Water goes through pipes to reach your kitchen and bathroom.

## pitch

To pitch a ball is to throw it. In baseball, the pitcher throws the ball to the batter.

To pitch is to set something up. You pitch a tent.

To pitch also means to fall forward or slope downward.

In music, pitch is the highness or lowness of a sound.

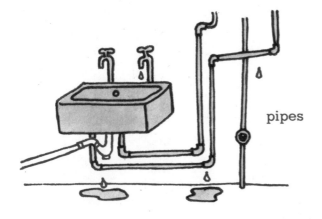

pipes

## pitcher

A pitcher is a container, usually with a handle and a spout, used for holding and pouring liquids.

## place

To place something is to put it somewhere.

A place is where something is or belongs.

## plain

Plain means ordinary, with nothing added. Mr. Greedy doesn't like plain cakes. He likes cakes covered with icing or cream.

Plain also means clear, easy to see or hear or understand.

A plain is a large, flat area of land.

## plan

To plan is to decide how you are going to do something before you start. Before his trip, Mr. Clever planned where he would be and what he would do every day.

## plane

A plane is a tool used to make wood smooth.

An airplane is called a plane.

## planet

A planet is a very large, heavenly body that moves around the sun. The earth is a planet.

planks

## plank

A plank is a flat length of wood. Mr. Muddle is trying to build a shed from planks of wood.

## plant

A plant is anything that grows in the ground. Trees and flowers are plants.

To plant is to put a seed or a small plant in the ground so that it will grow. Mr. Fussy plants his flowers in neat rows.

## plastic

Plastic is a material made by people and is used for making many things, such as cups and plates and containers of all kinds.

## plate

A plate is a flat dish that you put food on. Most plates are round.

platform

## platform

A platform is the raised part of a room or a building, higher than the rest of the floor. In a railroad station, you stand on the platform to wait for a train.

## play

To play is to do something that is fun. The children play outside.

To play also means to take part in a game, or to use a musical instrument.

A play is a story that is acted on a stage, on the radio or on television.

## pleasant

Something that is pleasant is something nice or that you enjoy.

## please

To please is to make someone happy. Mr. Chatterbox is always pleased to talk to someone.

Please is a polite word to say when you ask for something. "Pass me that pencil, please."

## plenty

Plenty means a lot of or as much as is needed.

## plug

A plug is a piece of rubber, plastic or wood used to block up a hole. Sinks have plugs to keep water from running down the drain.

An electrical plug connects a machine to an electricity supply.

## plum

A plum is a soft, round fruit with a large stone in the middle. Plums grow on trees.

## plump

To be plump is to be somewhat fat, well filled-out. Mr. Greedy is more than plump; he is fat. Little Miss Plump is just plump!

plums

## pocket

A pocket is like a small bag in your clothes that can hold things.

A pocketbook is like a small suitcase that people use to carry their money and other things.

## poem

A poem is a kind of writing that often uses words that rhyme.

## point

A point is the sharp end of something. Pins, needles, and sharp pencils have points.

To point is to show with a finger.

## poison

Poison is harmful. It will kill you or make you ill if you eat or drink it. Some berries and plants are poisonous.

## poke

To poke is to jab something sharply with a stick or finger.

## pole

A pole is a long, thin stick used to push, pull or support something.

The northern and southern points of the earth are called poles.

## policeman

A policeman helps and protects people and keeps people from breaking the law.

policeman

## polish

To polish something is to rub it until it shines. Mr. Fussy polishes his cups and plates when he washes them.

## polite

A polite person has good manners and is not rude. It is polite to say "Please" and "Thank you."

## pollution

Pollution is spoiling the air, sea, and land with unpleasant things like trash, smoke and leaking oil. The fumes from car engines pollute the air we breathe.

## pond

A pond is a small body of water. Some people have ponds in their gardens. Ponds are smaller than lakes.

pond

## pony

A pony is a small horse. Ponies are fun to ride.

## pool

A pool is an area of liquid. After the rain, there were pools of water on the lawn. Swimming pools are built for people to swim in.

### poor

Poor means having little money. Mr. Stingy pretends to be poor, but he has lots of money hidden away.

Poor also means unlucky or suffering. Poor Mr. Quiet couldn't get to sleep, because the wind was rustling the leaves.

Poor also means not very good. Mr. Clumsy is a poor ball player. He keeps dropping the ball!

### popular

Popular means liked by many people. Football is a popular sport.

### porcupine

A porcupine is a small animal with sharp spines, like needles, on its back.

### porridge

Porridge is a cereal made from oats. It is usually eaten in England.

### port

A port is a harbor or place where ships can take on or remove cargo, the goods they carry.

porridge

### portrait

A portrait is a picture of a person. Here is a portrait of Mr. Sneeze.

portrait

### position

The position of something is how or where it is. Mr. Bump fell head first into a hole. He stayed in that position until someone pulled him out.

position

### possessions

Your possessions are the things that you own. Mr. Strong packed all his possessions into two large trunks when he moved.

### possible

Possible means able to happen. It is possible to stand on the floor. It is not possible to stand on the ceiling, unless you are Mr. Impossible.

## post

A post is an upright piece of wood, metal or concrete that is placed in the ground.

To post also means to put something you want people to read in a place where they will see it. The notice was posted on the bulletin board.

## post office

A post office is the place where mail—letters, packages and postcards—is handled, and where you can buy stamps.

## poster

A poster is a large notice or picture placed on a wall.

## pot

A pot is a container to cook in or to hold food or other things. Mr. Wrong wears a flower pot for a hat.

## potato

A potato is a vegetable that grows in the ground. Potatoes are good to eat.

## pour

To pour is to make liquid flow from one place to another.

Mr. Wrong pouring tea

## powder

Powder is a very fine dust. It is made by crushing or grinding something. Flour is a powder something. Flour is a powder made by crushing grains of wheat or corn.

## power

Power is force or strength. Electricity provides power to make machines work. Mr. Strong has powerful muscles.

## practically

Practically means almost. When Mr. Busy and Mr. Slow had dinner together, Mr. Busy had practically finished his meal before Mr. Slow had eaten his first mouthful!

## practice

To practice is to do something over and over again until you can do it well. Tina practiced the piano every day.

## praise

To praise someone is to speak well of that person. Everyone praised Mr. Wrong when he came to the party on the right day.

## prayer

A prayer is what you say when you speak to God.

## precious

Precious means worth a lot. Gold is a precious metal.

### precisely

Precisely means exactly. According to Mr. Tall's clock, it is precisely five o'clock.

present

### present

A present is something you give to someone else. People give you presents on your birthday.

To be present means to be in this place, to be here.

The present time means now. Presently means soon.

### president

A president is one who is the head of a group, like the president of a club or company.

### press

To press is to push on something.

### pretend

To pretend is to make believe or to give a false appearance.

precisely

### prefer

To prefer is to like one thing better than something else. Mr. Greedy likes fruitcake, but he prefers chocolate cake. His preference is chocolate cake.

### prepare

To prepare is to get something ready. Mr. Happy prepared to have company. He cleaned his house, set the table and started the teapot. After these preparations, he waited for his guests to arrive.

Mr. Skinny pretending to be a ghost

## pretty

Pretty means pleasing to look at. Alison looked very pretty in her new party dress.

## prevent

To prevent something is to keep it from happening. The best way to prevent accidents is to be careful.

## price

The price of something is how much it costs. Mr. Grumpy grumbled that the price of cornflakes was too high.

## prick

To prick is to make a small hole with a sharp point.

## prince

A prince is the son of a king or queen.

## princess

A princess is the daughter of a king or queen.

printing press

## principal

The principal is the head or most important person in a place, as the principal of a school.

## principle

A principle is an accepted rule.

## print

To print is to put letters, words, or pictures on paper using a machine or a special tool. A newspaper is printed on a machine called a printing press.

## prison

A prison is a place where people who have broken the law are locked away. They are called prisoners.

## private

Something that is private is meant to be used or seen by the person to whom it belongs. If a door is marked "Private," it means that you should not go in without the owner's permission.

princess          prince

procession

### prize
A prize is something that you win in a contest or a game. Mr. Rush won a prize for winning the race.

### probably
Probably means very likely or almost certainly. Mr. Forgetful will probably forget something every time he goes shopping.

### problem
A problem is a very difficult question or situation. Mr. Bounce wondered how he could solve the problem of his bouncing.

### proceed
To proceed is to go on to do something. After a full breakfast, Mr. Greedy proceeded to eat a whole chocolate cake.

### procession
A procession is a large number of people or vehicles moving along together in a long line. When the circus came to town, brass bands, clowns and acrobats marched in the procession.

### produce
To produce something is to make it or to bring it into being. The factory in our town produced shoes. Tennis shoes are its main product.

### program
A program is something that is shown on television, heard on the radio or presented to an audience.

A program is also a list of people in a play, or of the music played or sung in a concert.

# O P Q R S T U V W X Y Z

## progress
Progress means moving ahead, developing, or improving. Mr. Grumpy made slow progress when he was learning to smile.

## promise
To promise is to give your word that you will do something. People are expected to keep their promises and not break them.

## proof
Proof is something that shows that a fact is true.

## proper
Proper means the right or the most suitable. Mr. Noisy didn't have the proper tool, so he used his shoe to hammer a nail into the wall!

## protect
To protect something means to keep it from harm. Mr. Nervous built a wall around his house to protect it from burglars. He thought the wall was good protection.

proud

protect

## proud
When you are proud of something, you are very pleased with it. Mr. Clever is very proud of his new invention. It is a machine that not only washes and dries clothes, but also irons them and puts them away!

## prove
To prove is to show that something is true. You can prove that the Mr. Men and Little Misses are in this book by looking at them yourself!

## provide

To provide means to give something that is needed. Cows provide us with milk, and sheep provide us with wool.

## prune

A prune is a dried plum. It is dark brown with a wrinkled skin.

To prune is to cut off branches from a tree, bush or hedge.

## pry

To pry is to be nosey. Mr. Nosey is always prying into other people's affairs by asking questions and looking through keyholes.

## public

Public means belonging to all the people, open to all, like a public park.

## pudding

A pudding is a sweet, thick food that you eat. Puddings can be hot or cold.

## puddle

A puddle is a small pool of water. There are puddles of water in the road after a heavy rain.

## pull

To pull is to try to move something towards you.

## pump

A pump is a machine used to force liquid or gas into something. A bicycle pump is used to fill a bicycle tire with air.

## pumpkin

A pumpkin is a large orange vegetable that grows on a vine. You carve pumpkins on Halloween to make jack-o-lanterns.

pump

## punch

To punch is to hit someone or something with your fist, or to make a hole in something.

Punch is a fruit drink.

## punish

To punish someone is to make him suffer because he or she has done something wrong. The giant punished Mr. Greedy for being greedy.

puddle

puppet

## pupil

A pupil is a student.

The pupil is the black part of the eye, that helps you see light.

## puppet

A puppet is a small doll or toy animal that can be made to move.

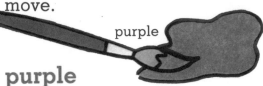

purple

## purple

Purple is a color that is a mixture of blue and red.

## purpose

A purpose is a reason. When you do something on purpose, you mean to do it.

## purse

A purse is a small bag used to carry money and other small objects.

## push

To push is to press hard on something to make it move away from you. When Mr. Funny's car broke down, Mr. Strong pushed it all the way home.

## put

To put something is to set it down or to place it. Mr. Clever put his books on the shelf.

## puzzle

A puzzle is something that is difficult to do or solve. Mr. Dizzy spent all week trying to do a crossword puzzle. By the end of the week he'd only solved one clue. And that was wrong!

## pyramid

A pyramid is a shape that has a square bottom and four sides shaped like triangles. The triangles meet in a point at the top. In ancient Egypt, huge pyramids of stone were built in honor of past kings and queens.

pyramid

## quack
Quack is the sound a duck makes.

## quality
Quality tells the worth or grade of something. Mr. Fussy only buys things of good quality.

## quantity
The quantity is the amount or number of something. Mr. Greedy eats a large quantity of baked goods every week.

## quarrel
To quarrel is to argue and to disagree. The children quarrelled about who should ride the bicycle first.

## quarter
A quarter is a piece of money that is worth 25 cents. Two dimes and a nickel equal a quarter.

If you divide something into four equal parts, each part will be a quarter of the whole thing.

## queen
A queen is a woman who rules a country or is the wife of a king.

## queer
Something that is queer is strange or unusual. Mr. Nonsense does some very queer things.

## question
A question is something that you ask to get an answer. Mr. Forgetful forgot the answer to the question.

quarter

## quick

Quick means fast or taking only a very short time. Mr. Busy does everything very quickly. It only takes him half a minute to mow his lawn.

quick

## quiet

Something that is quiet makes hardly any noise. Mr. Quiet does not have a loud voice. He talks so quietly that nobody hears him!

## quit

To quit is to stop. Mr. Lazy quit mowing the lawn after about half a minute.

## quite

Quite means completely. It is quite clear that we cannot finish this work today.

Quite also means rather. Mr. Bounce and Mr. Small are quite small.

quite

## quiver

To quiver is to shake and tremble. Mr. Nervous quivers when he is frightened, just like jelly quivers when you shake it!

quiver

## quiz

A quiz is a test, such as a spelling quiz.

rabbit

## rabbit
A rabbit is a small animal with long ears and a short, fluffy tail.

## race
A race is a contest to see who can do something in the fastest time.

To race is to move very fast.

## racket
A racket is a light bat with cord-like material stretched across it, such as a tennis racket.

A racket is also a loud noise.

## radiator
A radiator gives out heat to warm a room. Hot water or steam runs through metal pipes to keep the radiator warm.

radiator

## radio
A radio receives sounds that come through the air without using wires. You can listen to music and to people talking on the radio.

rag

## rag
A rag is a piece of torn or worn out cloth. People use rags for cleaning things. A puppy likes to tear things into rags!

railroad

## railroad
A railroad is the tracks that trains run on. It is also all the trains and buildings and people that make the company work.

## rain

Rain is the drops of water that fall from clouds in the sky. It rained yesterday, and it is raining again today.

## rainbow

A rainbow is a curve of colored light in the sky. You see a rainbow when it is raining and the sun is shining at the same time. There are seven colors in a rainbow. They are red, orange, yellow, green, blue, indigo and violet.

rainbow

## raise

To raise something means to lift it up. Jack raised his hand to show that he knew the answer to the teacher's question.

## rake

A rake is a garden tool with a long handle. It has a row of spikes which look like teeth at one end. A rake is used to gather leaves or grass and to make the soil smooth and even.

rake

## rapid

Rapid means very quick. When Mr. Mischief has been up to one of his tricks, he runs away rapidly so that he will not get caught.

## rare

Rare means not often seen or found. A four-leaf clover is rare. You will be lucky if you find one.

rare

## rash

A rash is a large number of tiny red spots on your skin. A rash can itch.

## raspberry

A raspberry is a small, soft red fruit. Raspberries grow on bushes.

raspberry

## rat

A rat is a long-tailed animal similar to a mouse, but larger.

## rather

Rather means quite. Mr. Mischief gave Mr. Chatterbox a rather unusual hat. It was filled with jam!

Rather also means liking one thing more than another thing. Mr. Lazy would rather sleep all day than go out.

## rattle

To rattle is to make several short, sharp sounds. The wind made the doors and windows of the house rattle. Mr. Nervous thought the house would fall down.

A rattle is a baby's toy that makes a noise when it is shaken.

## raw

Raw means not cooked. Carrots can be eaten raw or cooked.

## reach

To reach means to stretch out and touch. Mr. Tickle can reach around corners with his extraordinarily long arms. He is reaching through the window to tickle the teacher.

To reach also means to get to. It took Mr. Topsy-Turvy an hour to reach the station. He was slow getting there because he walked backwards!

read

## read

To read is to look at and understand words that are written down. Mr. Clever has read every book in the library. Twice!

To read also means to say out loud something that is written down.

## ready

Ready means able or prepared to start. Mr. Busy called for Mr. Slow to go shopping, but Mr. Slow wasn't ready. He had to get his hat and coat.

## real

Real means true and not false. Paper flowers are not real, but flowers growing in the garden are.

## realize

To realize means to understand clearly. Mr. Dizzy wondered why his living room seemed darker than usual. Then he realized he had forgotten to open the curtains!

## reason

The reason for something is why it happens. The reason Mr. Bump is always wearing bandages is that he keeps hurting himself.

reach

receive

## receive
To receive is to be given something. Mr. Quiet received an invitation to Mr. Happy's party.

## recent
Something recent is something that has happened not long ago.

## recipe
A recipe tells you how to cook something.

## recognize
To recognize is to know someone or something you have seen before.

## record
You play a record on a record player and it produces sound.

A record is also the very best known performance of something. Mr. Rush could set a world record for working fast.

## recorder
A recorder is a musical instrument like a flute.

A tape recorder is a machine that can make a record of sounds on a tape that you can play back to hear again and again.

## recover
To recover means to get better after an illness or a shock.

## rectangle
A rectangle is a four-sided figure, with the opposite parallel sides matching.

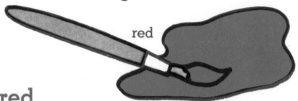

red

## red
Red is the color of a ripe tomato. Mr. Muddle wears a red hat.

## reduce
To reduce is to make smaller or less.

## refer
To refer to something means to direct attention to that thing.

## reflect
A shiny surface, like a mirror, reflects what is in front of it. Trees are reflected in the water.

reflect

## refrigerator
Food is stored inside a refrigerator to keep it cool and fresh.

## refuse
To refuse is to say no to something or not allow it. Mr. Grumpy refused to let anyone borrow his lawn mower.

## register
To register is to put your name on a list for something. The teacher checked the names of all the children registered for school.

## regret
To regret is to be sorry or to wish that something had not happened. Mr. Dizzy regretted leaving the gate open. The sheep got out, and the farmer was angry.

## rehearse
To rehearse is to practice. Actors usually have several rehearsals before they perform a play in front of an audience.

regret

## reindeer
A reindeer is a large deer that lives in cold places. Male reindeer have antlers.

## relate
To relate is to tell something, like a story or an experience.

To relate to something is to have a connection with it. The people related to you are the people in your family. They are called your relations or your relatives.

## relax
To relax is to rest and let your body feel at ease. Mr. Lazy likes to relax all day.

## release
To release something means to let it go free. The boy released the bird that was trapped inside his room. He opened the window and let it fly away.

## relief
Relief is a feeling of ease or pleasure that something bad is over or is not going to happen. It was a relief for Mr. Nervous to wake up from his terrible dream.

register

## rely

To rely on means to depend on. When someone tells you a secret they rely on you not to tell anyone else.

## remain

To remain means to stay the same.

To remain also means to be left. There were four cookies on the plate. John ate three and one remained.

## remarkable

Remarkable means unusual and worth noticing. Mr. Impossible can do some remarkable things, such as walking up the side of a tree!

remarkable

## remember

To remember is to keep something in your mind and not forget it.

## remind

To remind is to help someone remember something.

## remove

To remove is take away or take off.

## rent

To rent something is to use it for a time and pay for using it. To rent is also to allow something you own to be used and paid for.

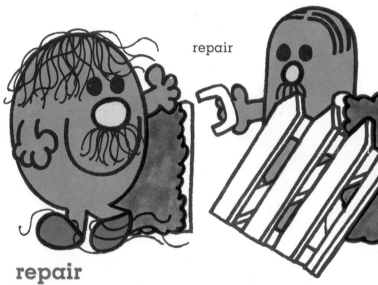

repair

## repair

To repair is to mend something and make it useful again. Mr. Fussy had to repair his gate after Mr. Clumsy had broken it.

## repeat

To repeat is to say or do something again. Mr. Quiet often has to repeat what he has said because people cannot hear him the first time.

replace

## replace

To replace is to put something back where it belongs. You must replace the lid on the cookie jar to keep the cookies fresh.

To replace also means to put one thing in place of another. Mr. Mischief stole the wizard's magic wand and replaced it with a broomstick.

## reply

To reply is to answer either by speaking or writing. When Mr. Tall received an invitation to a party he replied right away. He wrote to say he would love to go.

## report

A report is a description of something that has happened or has been done. Your teacher writes a report about your work.

## request

A request is something that has been asked for. To request means to ask for something.

## require

To require something is to need it. Someone who is sick requires medical care.

## rescue

To rescue is to save someone from harm or danger.

## respect

To respect is to admire someone and behave well towards that person.

## respond

To respond is to give an answer in words or by action.

## responsible

Responsible means taking care of something or having made something happen. The teacher asked who was responsible for breaking the window.

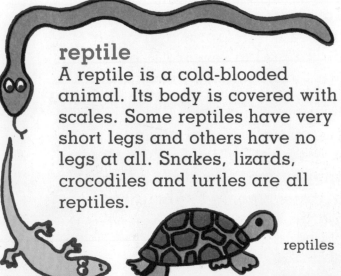

## reptile

A reptile is a cold-blooded animal. Its body is covered with scales. Some reptiles have very short legs and others have no legs at all. Snakes, lizards, crocodiles and turtles are all reptiles.

reptiles

responsible

### rest

To rest is to sit or lie down and be still for a while. Mr. Busy never has time to rest. He always finds another job to do.

The rest means what is left over. Mr. Skinny ate a few crumbs of his doughnut and gave the rest to Mr. Greedy.

### restaurant

A restaurant is a place where you pay to eat a meal. Mr. Uppity often eats in a restaurant.

restaurant

### result

The result is what happens because of something else.

A result is also the final score in a game or the grade on a test.

### return

To return is to go back to where you came from.

To return also means to give back. If you borrow a pencil you should return it as soon as you have finished using it.

### reveal

To reveal is to show something that has been hidden. Mr. Jones picked up a leaf and revealed Mr. Small hiding under it.

reveal

### revenge

Revenge is paying someone back for a wrong that has been done to you. The pig and elephant made fun of Mr. Dizzy. Later, Mr. Dizzy got his revenge by playing tricks on them.

### reverse

To reverse is to go or face in the opposite direction.

### revolution

A revolution is a complete change, such as the overthrow of an established government.

revenge

### revolve

To revolve is to turn around and around in one place.

### reward

A reward is given in return for help or bravery. The boy received a reward for finding the lost dog.

### rhyme

Words that rhyme sound like each other. "Cat" rhymes with "hat." "Sit" rhymes with "kit."

ribbon

## ribbon

A ribbon is a long, narrow piece of colored cloth. A ribbon is used to tie things together.

## rice

Rice is a plant that produces grain that we eat. Rice comes from hot countries and grows in fields of water called rice paddies.

## rich

Rich means having a lot of money or goods.

## rid

To get rid of means to be free of something by throwing it away or destroying it. Mr. Clever invented a new kind of mousetrap to get rid of the mice in his shed.

rid

## ride

To ride is to travel on an animal or in a vehicle. Many people ride in cars, and some people ride on horses. Mr. Clever has ridden on many different animals. In Africa, he rode on an elephant.

ridiculous

## ridiculous

Ridiculous means really silly. In Nonsenseland people do ridiculous things like putting wallpaper on the outside of their houses!

## right

Right means correct and not wrong. Joe had a high mark in the test because he got all the answers right.

Right also means the side opposite to the left. Mr. Noisy holds his pencil in his right hand.

right

## ring

To ring is to make the sound of a bell. A bell rang. Mr. Wrong opened the door, but it was the telephone that had rung.

A ring is a circular object that people wear on their fingers.

## rip

To rip something is to tear it roughly. Mr. Grumpy ripped the pages out of a book.

## ripe

Ripe means fully grown and ready for eating. Most fruits change color as they ripen.

## rise

To rise means to go up. The sun rises in the east. We watched as it rose over the treetops. By noon it had risen high in the sky.

To rise also means to get up from lying down, sitting or

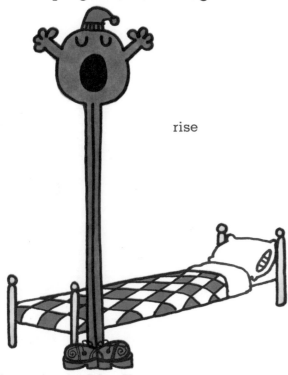

rise

kneeling. Mr. Tall stretches his legs when he rises from bed.

## risk

A risk is a chance of danger. If you go out without a raincoat when it looks like rain, you risk getting wet.

## river

A river is a large amount of water that always moves toward a sea or a lake.

river

## road

A road is a wide hard strip of land made for going from place to place. Roads are also called highways, freeways and turnpikes.

## roam

To roam is to travel or walk around with no purpose.

## roar

To roar is to make a loud, deep, harsh sound. Thunder roars and so does a lion.

To roar with laughter is to laugh very loudly.

## roast

To roast is to cook food in an oven or over a fire. We had roast meat for Sunday lunch.

## rob

To rob is to steal something from another person. There was a robbery at the bank last week. Robbers robbed the safe and took all the money.

## rock

A rock is a large lump of stone. Mr. Strong is so strong, he can pick up a rock in one hand and balance it on his head!

To rock is to move gently from side to side or back and forth. Mr. Lazy likes to rock back and forth in his rocking chair.

## rocket

A rocket is a firework that shoots up into the air very quickly.

A rocket is also a type of spaceship.

## rod

A rod is a long thin bar of wood, metal or other material.

## roll

To roll is to move along by turning over and over. Balls and wheels roll easily because they are round.

A roll is something rolled up, as a bed roll.

A roll is also a list, such as the roll the teacher has of everyone in the class.

A roll is also a type of bread.

## roof

A roof is the top covering of a building. Most houses have sloping roofs so that the rain can run off.

## room

A room is part of the inside of a house or building. A room has walls, a floor and a ceiling.

Room also means space. Mr. Clever has so many books, there is not room for another one on his bookshelf.

## rooster

A rooster is a male chicken.

## root

The root is the part of a plant that grows under the ground. The roots of a plant hold it firmly in the ground and take in food from the soil. Carrots are the roots of the carrot plant.

rocket

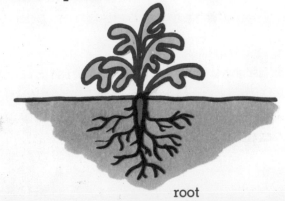

root

rope

## rope

A rope is strong, thick string. Rope is used for tying up or pulling heavy objects. A rope is also used for skipping.

rose

## rose

A rose is a sweet-smelling flower with a prickly stem. Roses grow on bushes in gardens and can be many different colors.

## rot

To rot is to go bad. Food rots if it is left around for a long time. Mr. Greedy's food never has time to become rotten.

## rough

Rough means not smooth. Sandpaper feels rough if you rub your fingers over it. The sea is very rough during a storm.

## round

Round means shaped like a circle or a ball. Mr. Happy, Mr. Bounce, and Mr. Small all are round.

## row

A row is a line of things or people. Seats in a theater are arranged in rows.

To row is to push a boat along with oars.

round

## royal

Royal means having to do with kings and queens. Kings and queens are royalty.

## rub

To rub is to wipe hard with something and move it back and forth over a surface. Mr. Fussy rubbed Mr. Messy's dirty fingermarks off the door with a damp cloth.

## rubber

Rubber comes from the sap of the rubber tree. Car tires are made of rubber. Mr. Bounce bounces like a rubber ball.

A rubber band is a small piece of rubber that stretches and is used to hold things together.

## rubbish

Rubbish is another word for trash, things that are useless or worn out or not wanted.

## rude

Rude means bad-mannered and not polite. Mr. Uppity is often rude. Instead of saying "Excuse me," he rudely pushes people out of the way.

## rug

A rug is a mat used to cover part of a floor. The cat curled up on a rug in front of the fire.

## ruin

To ruin is to spoil something so it is of no use at all. Mr. Forgetful's cakes were ruined. He forgot to take them out of the oven in time.

A ruin is what is left of an old building. In some parts of the world you can see the ruins of castles that were built hundreds of years ago.

rug

## rule

A rule tells you what you are supposed to do. When you play a game, you should follow the rules.

To rule also means to be at the head of a country. The king ruled for twenty years.

## ruler

A ruler is a length of wood, metal or plastic that is used for measuring and drawing straight lines. Mr. Clever used a ruler to draw an exact picture of his house.

## run

To run is to move quickly on foot. Running is faster than walking. Mr. Busy runs everywhere.

To run also means to work, like a clock or a motor.

run

## rush

To rush is to go very fast or do things very quickly. Mr. Rush never has time to finish anything, because he always rushes off to do something else.

## rust

Rust is a red coating that forms on metals like iron or steel when they have been allowed to get wet. If you leave your bike out in the rain it may get rusty.

## rye

Rye is a grain, used for bread and cereal.

## sack

A sack is a large bag made of thick, strong material. You can carry heavy things like potatoes and coal in sacks.

## sad

Sad means unhappy. When you are sad you don't feel like smiling or laughing.

## saddle

A saddle is a leather seat. You sit in a saddle when you ride a horse.

## safe

Safe means out of danger or free from harm.

saddle

## sail

A sail is a strong cloth fixed to a mast of a boat. The wind blows the sail and pushes the boat along. A sailor works on a boat.

## salad

A salad is a mixture of food that you eat cold.

## salary

Salary is money paid for doing work.

sail

## sale

A sale is selling something, or having something to sell.

## salt

Salt is like fine, white sand. Salt comes from sea-water or from underground mines. We sprinkle salt on our food to make it tasty.

## salute

To salute is to show respect by some special act, such as a salute to the flag.

189

same

### same
The same means exactly alike. Mr. Noisy's shoes are both the same color, but Mr. Wrong's are quite different.

### sand
Sand is made up of tiny grains of crushed rocks. There are miles of sandy beaches at the seaside.

### sandwich
A sandwich is two pieces of bread with a filling in between. Mr Strong loves egg sandwiches.

### satellite
A satellite is a body or device which moves in orbit around another larger body.

sandwich

### satisfy
To satisfy means to be good enough. Martin's teacher was satisfied with his work, so she gave him a good mark.

### sauce
Sauce is a thick liquid that you eat with food to make it more tasty. Mr. Nonsense put tomato sauce on his apple pie!

### saucepan
A saucepan is a cooking pot with a handle and usually a lid.

### saucer
A saucer is a small, shallow dish.

### sausage
A sausage is a roll of minced meat inside a thin skin case.

sausage

### save
To save is to take out of danger. Sailors pulled Mr. Bump from the sea to save him from drowning.

To save also means to keep something. Michael saves money every week. When he has saved enough money, he will buy a new football. He puts his money in a savings bank.

saw

## saw

A saw is a tool for cutting hard materials like wood and metal.

## say

To say is to speak. The grocer didn't hear what Mr. Quiet said. Mr. Quiet says everything very quietly.

## scale

A scale is a machine for weighing things.

## scare

To scare means to frighten. Any unusual sound scares Mr. Nervous.

## scarf

You wear a scarf around your neck or your head to keep you warm.

scarf

## scatter

To scatter means to throw or drop small pieces of something all over the place. Mr. Clumsy scattered cornflakes on the floor.

## schedule

A schedule is a list of times telling when things are planned to happen.

scissors

## school

School is a place where people go to learn.

## science

Science is the study of how things work and why things happen.

## scissors

A pair of scissors has two sharp blades fixed together. Scissors are used for cutting.

## score

The score is the number of points or goals made by each team or player in a game.

## scrap

A scrap is a small piece of something. Sally wrote down Sue's telephone number on a scrap of paper.

## scratch

To scratch something is to make a mark on it with a sharp or pointed object.

To scratch also means to rub something that itches.

## scream

To scream is to make a very loud noise because you are frightened or hurt. The baby screamed when she heard a loud noise.

## screen

A screen is made of wire and used on windows and doors as protection to keep insects out.

A screen is also the surface on which you see movies and television.

## screw

A screw is a kind of nail or pin that turns to hold things together.

scrub

## scribble

To scribble is to write in a messy or aimless way.

## scrub

To scrub is to clean something by rubbing it very hard. Mr. Fussy is scrubbing his floor with a brush.

## sea

The sea is the salt water that covers most of the earth. Ships sail across the sea to different countries.

seal

## seal

A seal is an animal that lives in and near the sea. Seals have flippers instead of legs to help them swim.

To seal something means to close it. You seal the edge of an envelope.

## search

To search means to try and find something by looking very carefully for it. Mr. Chatterbox searched the house for his shoes, but Mr. Mischief had hidden them in the garden!

## season

A season is a particular time of the year. The year is divided into four seasons. Spring, summer, autumn and winter are seasons.

## seat

A seat is something to sit on. Chairs and benches and stools and sofas all have seats.

seasons

## second

Second means coming after the first. Mr. Busy was second in the running race. Mr. Rush was first.

second

A second is also a very short length of time. There are 60 seconds in a minute.

## secret

A secret is something that is known to some people but not to others. When you are told a secret, you must keep it to yourself and not tell anyone else.

## see

To see is to look at things with your eyes. Jim sees a bird in the tree. He saw the same bird yesterday. He has seen it every-day this week.

To see is also to understand.

## seed

A seed is the small part of a plant that will grow into a new plant.

## seek

To seek is to try to find something or someone.

## seem

To seem means to appear to be.

## select

To select means to choose. Every day you select what you will wear.

## selfish

Selfish means interested in yourself and not caring about others.

## sell

To sell is to exchange something for money. Allan sells books. Yesterday he sold dictionaries to a school.

## send

To send means to make something or someone go from one place to another. Mother sent Emily to the store for apples.

## sense

To sense something is to become aware of it or feel it through seeing, hearing, smelling, tasting or touching.

Sense is good practical intelligence. It doesn't make sense to walk in the rain without opening your umbrella. It is not a sensible thing to do.

sense

## sentence

A sentence is a number of words put together so that they mean something.

A sentence is also the punishment given to a criminal.

## separate

Separate means not together. Mr. Silly and Mr. Nonsense live in separate houses.

To separate is to take apart.

## series

A series is a number of things of the same kind or that come one after another. A television series is a number of programs about the same people or things.

## serious

Serious means not funny and not to be treated as a joke. The wizard was serious when he told Mr. Mischief to stop playing tricks.

## serve

To serve is to give food, to help or to be useful. When you go to a restaurant or a store, you like to get good service.

To serve also means to do duty to your country, as in the army or navy or in Congress.

## set

To set means to put something in a place or in a position, such as setting the table for dinner or setting a clock.

A set is a group of things that belong together.

## several

Several means quite a few.

## sew

To sew is to join pieces of cloth together with a needle and thread.

## sex

Sex means being male or female.

## shade

The shade is where it is darker because there is not as much light. It is darker in the shade of the tree than in the sunlight.

A shade is a window covering to keep the light out.

## shadow

A shadow is the dark shape made on the ground or on a wall when someone or something is in front of a light.

shadow

## shake

To shake is to move something quickly from side to side or up and down. Mr. Stingy shook his money box to see how much money was inside.

To shake also means to tremble all over. Mr. Nervous shakes when he is frightened.

shape

## shall

Shall means will. What shall I do?

## shape

The shape is the outer form of anything. The shape of Mr. Strong's body is square.

## share

To share something is to give other people parts of it, or to let other people use it. Mr. Happy is sharing his birthday cake.

share

## sharp

Sharp means having a pointed end or an edge that cuts. It is easy to cut paper with sharp scissors. You need a sharp pencil to draw a fine line.

## shave

To shave is to scrape something off with a sharp instrument. Daddy shaves every day.

## she

She means a female. She is my sister.

## shed

A shed is a small wooden or metal building for keeping things, such as tools and bicycles, in.

To shed is to lose or come off. Some dogs shed their hair.

sheep

## sheep

A sheep is an animal that has a wooly coat. Sheep are kept on farms.

## sheet

A sheet is a large piece of cloth that is used on a bed.

A sheet is also a piece of paper. You write a letter on a sheet of paper.

## shelf          shelf

A shelf is a flat board placed inside a cupboard or a closet or on a wall. You put things like books or food or cups on shelves.

## shell

A shell is a hard covering. Eggs and nuts have shells. Turtles, snails, and other sea creatures also have shells.

## shelter

A shelter is a place where people or animals are protected in bad weather. When it rains, a bus shelter keeps people dry while they are waiting for a bus.

## shine

To shine means to give off light. A street lamp shines at night so that people can see where to walk.

To shine also means to polish something to a mirror-like finish, to make it shiny.

## ship

A ship is a large boat that sails on the sea. Ships are used to carry people or goods across the ocean.

## shirt

A shirt is a piece of clothing. It has sleeves and a collar and buttons up the front. Mr. Muddle puts his shirt on backwards.

shiver

## shiver

To shiver means to shake because you are cold or frightened. Mr. Sneeze lives in Shivertown. Everyone there shivers all the time because it is so cold.

ship

## shock

Shock is a sudden feeling of fear or surprise. The mailman gave Mr. Quiet a shock by banging on his door.

To shock someone is to make him feel very angry or upset.

## shoe

You wear shoes on your feet. Shoes are made of leather or plastic and can be fastened with shoelaces or straps and buckles.

## shoot

To shoot means to fire a gun or an arrow to hit someone or something. The man shot two cans off the fence.

To shoot also means to aim a ball at a goal.

shoot

## shop

To shop is to go to the store to buy something. Mr. Greedy goes shopping for food everyday.

## shore

Shore is land at the edge of a lake, sea or ocean.

## short

Short means not long, or not tall. "Cat" is a short word. Everyone is shorter than Mr. Tall.

## should

If you should do something, you ought to do it. You should be careful crossing the street.

Should also means will. I should be finished with my homework soon.

shoulder

## shoulder

Your shoulders join your arms to your body. Mr. Small sat on Mr. Robinson's shoulder.

## shout

To shout is to call out loudly.

## shovel

A shovel is a tool for digging and lifting things. We shoveled snow.

## show

To show something means to let other people see it. Mr. Uppity has shown everyone his new watch.

To show also means to explain by doing something. Dad showed me how to make a model car.

A show is something entertaining, such as a play or a concert.

### shower

A shower is a light rain.

A shower is also a kind of bath. When you take a shower, you stand up and water is sprayed over you from above.

### shriek

To shriek is to cry out sharply in a loud, high voice. Mr. Small shrieked when Mr. Tickle tickled him.

### shrill

Shrill means making a sharp, high sound. An ambulance siren makes a shrill sound.

### shrink

To shrink means to get smaller. The King of the Goblins made Mr. Uppity shrink whenever he was rude to people.

### shy

A shy person is quiet and a bit frightened of other people. Little Miss Shy is so shy that she lives far away from anybody else.

### sick

Sick means ill, not well. Mr. Greedy sometimes feels sick after he has eaten too much.

### side

A side is one of the edges or surfaces of something. A square has four sides.

A side is also the part that is on the left or the right but not in the middle. Mr. Lazy has a table on one side of his bed and a chair on the other side.

If something is at your side, it is next to you.

shrink

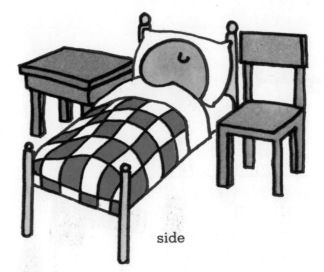

side

### shut

To shut means to close up so that nothing can get in or out. He shut the windows to keep the wind and rain out.

Shut also means not open. The door is shut.

### sigh

To sigh is to make a long, deep sound as you breathe out. People sigh when they are tired or upset or relieved.

### sight
Sight is seeing. Mr. Clever wears glasses to improve his sight.

A sight is something that is seen. A sunrise can be a beautiful sight. Mr. Messy is a sight to see!

sign

### sign
A sign gives you information or stands for something. There was a sign on the door saying, "No Dogs Allowed."

To sign means to write your name at the end of a letter or on a form.

### signal
A signal is something that warns you or tells you what to do. A red traffic light is a signal that tells drivers to stop.

### silent
Silent means having no sounds. Mr. Quiet likes silence.

### silly
Silly means not making sense. In Nonsenseland, birds fly backwards, which is really very silly.

Silly also means foolish. It is silly to eat too many cakes at a party, because you may make yourself sick.

### silver
Silver is a precious metal. It is grayish-white and shines when it is polished. Silver is used to make jewelry, cups and other things.

Silver is what we call the knives, forks, and spoons we eat with, even though they may be made of other things.

### similar
Similar means nearly the same. Mr. Happy and Mr. Bounce are similar. Both are round and yellow, but Mr. Bounce is smaller than Mr. Happy and wears a red hat.

similar

simple

## simple

Simple means easy. Mr. Muddle cannot do even a simple job right. Look how he hammers a nail into the wall.

## since

Since means after, or between a time in the past and now. Mr. Bounce has stopped bouncing all over the place since he started wearing heavy boots.

## sing

To sing is to make musical sounds with your voice. You sing a song. A choir is a group of people singing together. I sang with a choir once.

sing

## single

Single means one. There wasn't a single cookie left on the plate after Mr. Greedy had finished his tea.

## sink

To sink means to drop down to the bottom of a liquid. A stone will sink if you throw it into a pond. A piece of wood will float.

A sink is also a deep basin that holds water. A kitchen sink is used to wash dishes.

A stone will sink if you throw it into the water.

## sip

To sip means to drink something by taking a little at a time. You can taste a drink by sipping it.

## sister

Your sister is a girl or woman who has the same mother and father as you.

## sit

To sit is to put the lower part of your body down. Bill sat in the baby's chair. The baby was sitting on his mother's lap.

ice skating

## size

The size of something is how big it is. It helps to know what size your feet are when you go to buy shoes.

## skate

To skate means to move on skates.

Skates are specially made to wear on your feet so that you can slide along. Ice skates have metal blades on them, and roller skates have wheels.

## skeleton

A skeleton is the framework of bones inside a person or animal. We saw the skeleton of a dinosaur at the museum.

## skin

Skin is the outer covering of the body of a person or animal. The skin of most animals is covered with fur or hair.

Skin is also the outer covering of fruit. Before you eat a banana, you have to peel off the skin.

## skinny

Skinny means very thin. Mr. Skinny is so thin you can hardly see him when he turns sideways.

skinny

## skip

To skip means to run or jump lightly, hopping from one foot to the other.

To skip also means to do without, such as skipping a meal.

## skirt

A skirt is a part of a dress or a separate piece of clothing that hangs from the waist.

### sky
The sky is the air above us. On a sunny day the sky is blue. When it rains, the sky is gray and cloudy.

### slam
To slam a door means to shut it with a loud bang. Mr. Noisy never shuts doors quietly. He is always slamming them.

### slap
To slap is to hit with the open hand and make a sharp noise. Mother slapped John's hand because he took the baby's toy.

### sled
A sled is a small light cart that runs over snow. It has pieces of metal or wood on the bottom to slide over snowy ground.

sled

### sleep
When you sleep you close your eyes and are not awake. You rest your mind and body completely. When you are tired or sleepy, all you want to do is go to bed and sleep. After you have slept, you feel rested.

### sleeve
Sleeves are the parts of clothing that cover your arms. Coats and shirts have sleeves. Long sleeves come right down to your wrist, but short sleeves end above your elbow.

### slice
A slice is a flat piece that has been cut from something like bread or cheese or meat. Mr. Greedy cuts several slices of bread for his breakfast.

slice

### slide
To slide means to move along smoothly. You can slide on something slippery, like ice or a newly polished floor.

A slide is for playing on. It has a smooth slope for sliding down and a ladder to climb back up to the top. Mr. Rush slid very fast.

### slip
To slip is to slide on something by accident. Mr. Bump slips all over the place. Yesterday he slipped on the steps. Today he slipped on a banana peel.

A slip is an article of clothing worn under dresses.

slipper

## slipper
A slipper is a soft shoe that you wear indoors.

## slippery
Slippery means very smooth and easy to slip on. Icy roads are slippery.

## slit
A slit is a long narrow opening. Mr. Nosey peeped through a slit in the fence.

## slope
A slope is a piece of ground that is not level. Mr. Funny parked his car on a slope and forgot to put the brake on. The car rolled right down the hill!

slope

## slow
Slow means taking a long time. Mr. Slow does everything slowly. It takes him all morning to eat his breakfast!

## slumber
To slumber is to sleep. Mr. Lazy slumbers in Sleepyland all day long.

## small
Small means not big. A mouse is a small animal. Mr. Small is even smaller than a mouse. He is so little you can hardly see him.

## smart
Smart means quick to learn. Mr. Clever is really very smart.

   Smart also means neatly dressed.

smash

## smash
To smash something is to break it into tiny pieces. Mr. Bump smashed a window while he was carrying a ladder.

## smell
You smell things with your nose. Roast chicken smells delicious! I smelled it cooking when I came home.

## smile

You smile when you feel happy or amused or friendly. When you smile the ends of your mouth turn upwards. Mr. Happy smiles. So does Little Miss Sunshine.

## smoke

Smoke is the gray cloud that comes from something that is burning. A log fire smokes when it burns.

## smooth

Smooth means flat and even and not bumpy. Glass has a very smooth surface.

## snail

snail

A snail is a small animal that has a hard shell on its back. It has a soft body and moves along very slowly.

## snake

A snake is a reptile with a long, thin body and no legs. It moves by sliding along the ground. Some snakes have poisonous bites, and some have beautiful, patterned bodies.

snake

## snap

To snap is to make a sudden sharp sound. Mr. Nervous jumped when he heard a twig snap.

A snap is also a fastener made of two pieces of metal or plastic that fit together, sometimes with a snapping sound.

## snatch

To snatch is to grab something quickly.

## sneeze

To sneeze is to make a sudden, loud noise through your nose. You sneeze a lot when you have a cold. Mr. Sneeze is always sneezing. A sneeze makes a sound like ATISHOO!

sneeze

## sniff

To sniff is to take a short breath through your nose. People sometimes sniff when they are crying or when they need a handkerchief. The dog sniffed at the biscuit to see if it smelled good enough to eat.

## snore

To snore is to make a noisy breathing sound when you are asleep. When Mr. Noisy snores, everyone for miles around can hear him.

snow

### snow

Snow is water in the air that has become frozen. It is soft and cold and white and falls from the sky in winter. When it snows, you can make snowballs and snowmen. Mr. Snow loves snow!

### so

So means too, as in also. Mr. Happy went shopping and so did Mr. Small.

So means very or in such a way. Mr. Quiet always speaks so softly that no one can hear him.

### soak

To soak something is to make it very wet. Mr. Clumsy was soaked when he fell into the pool with all his clothes on.

### soap

We use soap to wash ourselves and our clothes. Soap may be a solid lump, a powder or a liquid. Mr. Messy hates soap!

### sock

A sock is clothing that you wear on your foot and part of your leg. You put on socks before you put on your shoes.

To sock someone is to hit him hard.

### soft

Soft means not hard or firm. A pillow is soft. So is a furry kitten.

Soft also means quiet. It is the opposite of loud. Mr. Quiet has a soft voice. He speaks very softly.

soil

### soil

Soil is the soft brown surface of the land. Soil is also called earth. Plants are grown in soil. Mr. Topsy-Turvy dug a deep hole in the soil and planted a rose bush, upside down, of course!

### soldier

A soldier is a person who belongs to an army. Soldiers wear uniforms.

**solid**

Solid means hard all the way through. A solid piece of wood is not hollow inside.

**solve**

To solve a puzzle or problem is to find the answer. Mr. Muddle finally solved the mystery of his missing teapot. He had put it in the oven by mistake!

solve

**some**

Some means a number of something, but not very many. Some kids missed school today.

Some also means part of. Would you like some candy?

**son**

A son is a male child. Steven is the son of his parents.

**song**

A song is a piece of music with words that you can sing.

**soon**

Soon means in a short time.

sore

**sore**

Sore means painful. Mr. Bounce got a sore head when he bounced up and hit the ceiling.

**sorry**

You feel sad when you are sorry. When you have done something to hurt or annoy someone else, you are sorry and hope the person will forgive you.

**sort**

A sort is a kind. Chickens and lions are different sorts of animals.

To sort is to put things into groups of the same kind. Mr. Small is sorting his knives, forks, and spoons into separate piles so he can put them away.

sort

**sound**

A sound is a noise or anything you can hear. A sound can be very quiet, as when a pin falls on the floor, or very loud, as when we hear thunder.

### soup
Soup is liquid food. It is made by cooking vegetables or meat in water or milk.

### sour
Sour means having a sharp taste.

### south
South is a direction. South is toward the bottom of the earth. Florida is in the southern part of the United States.

### space
A space is a hole or a gap between things, like a space between words.

Space is room, an area. Mr. Greedy takes up a lot of space.

Space is also the whole universe. Astronauts travel through space to the moon.

spare

### spare
Spare means extra. Mr. Worry keeps a spare front door key under his mat, in case he loses his other key.

### sparkle
To sparkle is to shine with a bright light. Mr. Busy's windows sparkled in the sunshine when he had finished cleaning them.

sparrow

### sparrow
A sparrow is a small brown bird. You often see sparrows in the garden.

### speak
To speak is to say something. Nobody gets a chance to speak when Mr. Chatterbox is around. He spoke all night at a town meeting.

### special
Special means different from the rest, not usual. Mr. Topsy-Turvy has a special clock. It tells the time backwards!

space

### spade
A spade is a tool with a long handle that is used for digging.

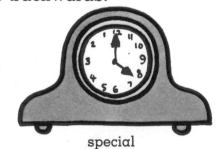
special

## speck

A speck is a very tiny bit. You will have to look very hard to find a speck of dust at Mr. Fussy's house. He dusts ten times a day!

speech

## speech

Speech is talking.

A speech is something special that is said in front of lots of people. Mr. Chatterbox is good at making speeches. One of his speeches lasted all day and all night!

## speed

Speed is how fast something or someone goes. Mr. Rush moves along at great speed. He is always speeding somewhere and getting nowhere!

## spell

To spell is to write or say the letters of a word in the right order. All the words in this book should be spelled correctly.

A spell is a magic word or rhyme. The King of the Goblins put a spell on Mr. Uppity. The spell made Mr. Uppity shrink every time he was rude.

## spend

To spend is to pay money to buy something. Mr. Greedy spent all his money at the bakery.

To spend also means to do something for a time. Mr. Daydream spends hours daydreaming.

spend

## spider

A spider is a small creature with eight legs. A spider spins a web to catch insects for food.

## spill

To spill is to make things fall accidentally out of a container. Mr. Clumsy is always spilling things. This morning he spilled his milk and his cereal.

## spin

To spin is to go around and around very quickly.

To spin also means to make a thread.

## spinach

Spinach is a vegetable with dark green leaves.

## spit

To spit is to push liquid or food out of the mouth.

## splash

To splash is to make water or other liquids fly all around.

## splendid

Splendid means wonderful. Little Miss Splendid has a high opinion of herself. She thinks she is splendid.

## splinter

A splinter is a thin, sharp piece of wood.

## split

To split is to break apart. Jim's trousers split when he sat down.

## spoil

To spoil something is to damage it.

## spoon

spoon

A spoon is a metal or wooden object with a handle and a round end. Spoons are used for cooking and eating.

## sport

A sport is a game or race played by using muscles. Swimming, football and tennis are sports.

spot

## spot

A spot is a particular place. This field looks like a good spot for a picnic.

A spot is also a small mark. A leopard has spots.

To spot means to catch sight of. Mr. Nosey spotted an ant walking along his wall. He doesn't miss a thing!

## spray

To spray is to wet somthing with tiny drops of liquid. Mr. Fussy sprays his roses every day.

spray

## spread

To spread is to cover a wide area. Mr. Silly spread ice cream on his bread!

A spread is a covering that goes over the blankets on a bed.

## spring

Spring is the time of year between winter and summer.

A spring is a piece of metal or plastic that jumps back into place after you have pressed it. There are springs inside some beds and chairs.

A spring is also a small stream of water.

To spring is to jump, as when a cat springs at a mouse.

To spring is also to grow from something. Flowers sprang up overnight.

## sprinkle

To sprinkle is to scatter small bits or drops of something. Mr. Muddle sprinkled sugar over his dinner instead of salt.

square

## square

A square is a shape that has four sides and corners. The sides of a square are all the same length. Mr. Strong is square.

## squash

To squash is to make something flat by pressing on it. Mr. Muddle squashed his hat when he sat on it by mistake.

Squash is a fruit that grows on vines. We usually eat squash as a vegetable.

## squeak

To squeak is to make a high, sharp sound. Bicycle wheels squeak if they need oiling.

## squeeze

To squeeze is to push on the sides of something. When Mr. Strong squeezed a tube of toothpaste, he pressed so hard that all the toothpaste came out.

sprinkle

## spy

To spy is to watch people secretly. Mr. Nosey spies on his neighbors by peeping through the curtains.

A person who spies on others is called a spy.

squeeze

## squirrel

A squirrel is a small mammal with a long, bushy tail. Squirrels live in trees and eat nuts.

## squirt

To squirt is to come forth in a rapid stream from an opening. Water squirts from a hose.

## stage

A stage is a raised platform at the front of a theater or hall. Plays are performed on stages so the audiences can see them clearly.

## stain

A stain is a dirty mark that is difficult to wash out. Mr. Messy's hands were covered with purple stains after he picked blackberries.

## stale

Stale means not fresh. Stale food is old and dried up and not very good to eat.

## stalk

A stalk is a plant stem, such as a stalk of celery.

stamp

stair

## stair

A stair is a step. Stairs reach from one level in a building to another.

## stamp

To stamp is to put your foot down very heavily and make a noise. Mr. Noisy stamps everywhere. Clump! Clump!

You stick a stamp on a letter or package to show that you have paid for it to be mailed.

## stand

To stand is to be upright. The opposite of stand is sit. Mr. Rush never stands still. He has never stood still for a whole minute.

stars

### star

A star is a bright object in space. We see stars as points of light in the sky at night.

A star is also a famous person, such as an actor or a singer.

### stare

To stare is to look hard at something for a long time.

### start

To start is to begin. Mr. Slow arrived at the theater after the play had already started.

### starve

To starve is to be without food for a long period of time.

### state

A state is an area of land within a country. A state is also all of the people who live in that area. There are fifty states in the United States of America.

A state is also the way a person or thing acts. Ice is water in a frozen state.

To state something is to say it. To make a statement is to say what you believe.

### station

A station is a place where trains or buses stop. Mr. Lazy fell asleep on the train and got off at the wrong station.

### stay

To stay is to remain in one place and not move away. Mr. Happy stayed on the beach all day.

To stay also means to visit a place and live there for a short time. Mr. Skinny stayed with Mr. Greedy for a few weeks to see if he could improve his appetite.

### steady

Steady means firm and not moving. Mr. Bump climbed his ladder without making sure it was steady. The ladder fell over and so did Mr. Bump!

Steady is also continuing, like a steady rain.

steam

### steal

To steal is to take something that belongs to someone else and not give it back. Robbers broke into the drug store and stole all the money.

### steam

Steam is cloudy moisture. When a pot of water boils, steam is formed.

steep

## steep

Steep means sloping very sharply uphill or downhill. Even Mr. Rush was out of breath after running up a steep hill.

## stem

A stem is a part of a plant. The flowers and leaves are attached to the stem. Most plants have long, thin stems that are green or brown. A stem is sometimes called a stalk.

stems

## step

To step is to lift up your foot and put it down again somewhere else. You take steps when you are walking or dancing or climbing.

A step is one stair, such as a step up to go into a house.

## stern

A stern person is firm and strict, and looks rather cross.

The stern is the back part of a ship.

## stew

To stew is to cook food very slowly in water.

Stew is a meal made from stewed meat and vegetables.

stick

## stick

A stick is a long, thin piece of something. The dog is carrying a stick of wood.

A stick can also be something that is shaped like a stick, such as carrot sticks or a stick of gum.

To stick is to fasten things together with glue, tape or paste. These things are sticky.

To stick is to make a hole with something sharp.

To stick also means to be attached, to be firm or to be caught unable to move. Mr. Clumsy got his shoe stuck in the mud.

## stiff

Stiff means hard and not easy to bend. New shoes sometimes feel very stiff until you have worn them for a while.

## still

Still means quiet and not moving. Mr. Busy never stands still for a second. He always has something to do.

Still also means up to the present time. Do you still belong to the swimming club?

stir

## stir

To stir is to mix by moving a spoon or other instrument around in it. Mr. Muddle stirred his tea with a pencil and wrote with a spoon!

## stitch

You make a stitch when you knit or sew.

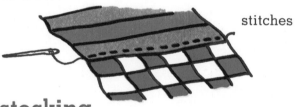

stitches

## stocking

A stocking is a piece of clothing that covers the foot and leg.

## stomach

Your stomach is the part of your body where your food goes after you have swallowed it.

## stone

Stone is a very hard substance. Rocks are pieces of stone.

A stone is also the hard seed inside some fruits like peaches and plums.

## stop

To stop is to finish moving. The taxi stopped at a traffic light.

To stop also means to finish doing something.

## store

A store is a place where you go to buy things.

To store something is to put it away to keep it. Mr. Fussy has a special storage closet.

## stork

A stork is a large bird with very long legs.

## storm

A storm is very bad weather. In a storm there may be a strong wind and heavy rain or thunder and lightning. The sea is very rough on a stormy day.

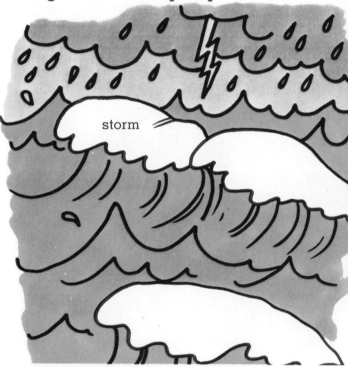

storm

## story

A story tells how something happened. Some stories are true but many are made up.

## stove

A stove makes heat using a fuel such as gas, electricity or coal. You use a stove for cooking or heating.

straight

## straight
Straight means not bent or curved. Mr. Clever draws a straight line with a ruler.

## strain
To strain is to stretch beyond the normal limit, to use great effort.

To strain is also to draw off liquid by holding back the solid parts of something.

## strange
Strange means odd or unusual. Mr. Topsy-Turvy has a strange way of talking.

## stranger
A stranger is a person who is not known to you.

## strap
A strap is a thin piece of leather used to fasten objects or hold them in place.

## straw
A straw is a thin tube through which liquid is sucked.

Straw is also the hollow stem of the wheat plant.

## strawberry
A strawberry is a soft, red, juicy fruit. Strawberries have their seeds on the outside.

## stream
A stream is a small river. Mr. Funny is fishing in a stream.

stream

## street
A street is a road in a town or city. Cars, buses and trucks ride on streets.

## strength
Strength is the power of being strong. Mr. Strong showed his strength by picking up a barn and carrying it above his head.

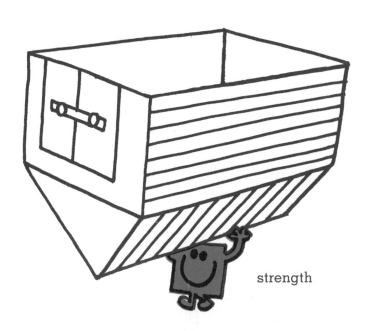

strength

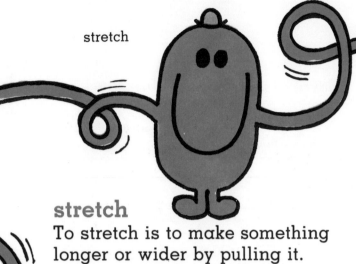

stretch

## stretch

To stretch is to make something longer or wider by pulling it. Elastic stretches when you pull it.

To stretch also means to reach out. Mr. Tickle can reach a long way when he stretches out his extraordinarily long arms.

## strict

A strict person makes sure you obey him or her. The swimming instructor was very strict. She made her pupils practice hard.

## strike

To strike is to hit hard. The builder struck the nail with his hammer.

To strike also means to light a match by rubbing it against a rough surface.

## string

String is strong thread that is used for tying things. Mr. Sneeze is tying a package with string.

string

## strip

A strip is a long, thin piece of something, such as tape.

To strip is to take off the covering of something, as in stripping a bed.

## stripe

A stripe is a narrow band of color. Mr. Snow's scarf has red and white stripes.

## stroke

To stroke is to move your hand gently over something. Jill stroked the cat, and it began to purr.

## strong

A strong person is powerful and can lift heavy things. Mr. Strong is so strong he can hammer nails into the wall just by tapping them with his finger!

## struggle

To struggle is to make a great effort to do something. Mr. Small struggled to lift a large pebble.

## stubborn

A stubborn person refuses to give in or change his mind. Mr. Stingy stubbornly refused to put his money in the bank.

## study

To study means to read or to learn about something. Jack studies every night. He studied so well that he got the highest mark in the class. Jack is a good student.

stupid

## stupid

Stupid means foolish or not clever. The pig thought Mr. Dizzy was stupid because he couldn't answer a simple question.

## submarine

A submarine is a ship that can travel under water.

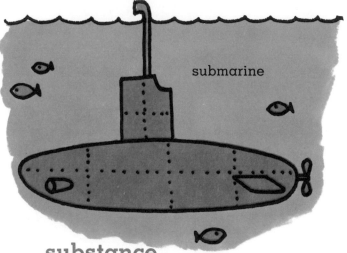

submarine

## substance

A substance is what something is made of. Stone is a very hard substance, and glue is a sticky, liquid substance.

## substitute

A substitute is a person or thing used in place of another. When Mr. Greedy cannot get chocolate cake, he will take a substitute.

## subtract

To subtract is to take a part away from a whole. When you subtract two from five, you have three.

## succeed

To succeed is to do what you have set out to do. Mr. Quiet succeeded in finding a job at the library. He became a success.

To succeed is also to follow in order. If a president dies, he is succeeded by the vice president.

## such

Such means very. Mr. Skinny is such a thin man.

## suck

To suck is to draw liquid into your mouth. You suck drinks through a straw. Sucking candy helps you get the flavor.

## sudden

Sudden means happening quickly, and not expected. Mr. Happy had a shock when his chair suddenly collapsed. Mr. Mischief had sawed through one of the legs!

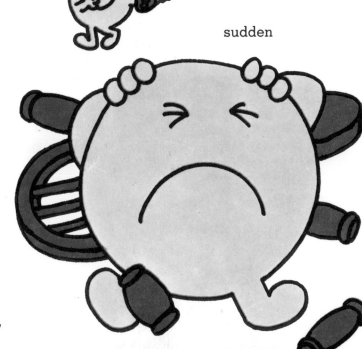

sudden

## suffer
To suffer is to feel great pain or sadness.

## sugar
Sugar is a substance that is added to other foods and drinks to make them sweeter. Sugar looks like very small grains of sand.

## suggest
To suggest is to give someone an idea. The doctor suggested to Mr. Skinny that staying with Mr. Greedy might improve his appetite. Mr. Skinny thought this was a good suggestion.

## suit
To suit is to be right for. Mr. Chatterbox thought his new hat suited him very well.

A suit is a set of clothes. A man's suit has a pair of trousers, a jacket and sometimes a vest.

## sum
A sum is an amount of something, like a sum of money. The sum of seven and three is ten.

suit

summer

## summer
Summer is the time of the year between spring and fall. Summer is usually the hottest time of the year.

## sun
The sun is a very large, hot, bright star in the sky. The sun gives us light and heat and is seen during the day. When the sun is shining, we say it is a sunny day.

## super
Super means extra special, more or greater than.

### supermarket

A supermarket is a very large store that sells all kinds of foods and goods. In a supermarket you put what you want to buy into a cart and pay at the checkout counter.

### supper

Supper is another word for dinner. Mr. Silly has cornflakes on toast for his supper, with a cup of warm ice cream!

supper

### supply

To supply means to provide things that are wanted or needed.

Supplies are things that are needed and used up, such as soap and food.

### support

To support is to hold up. A table is supported by four legs.

To support also means to take care of, to supply what is needed.

### suppose

To suppose is to think something will happen. I suppose it will rain when we get to the beach.

To be supposed to do a thing is to be expected to do it.

surface

### sure

Sure means certain and having no doubt. Mr. Worry is always sure something terrible will happen.

### surface

The surface is the top or outside of something. The surface of the road was very bumpy.

### surname

Your surname is your last name. Roger Hargreaves' surname is Hargreaves.

surname

## surprise

A surprise is something that you do not expect to happen. A surprise can be nice or unpleasant. Mr. Greedy had a surprise when he bit into the cake Mr. Mischief had sent him. It was made of cotton and toothpaste!

## surround

To surround something is to be on all sides of it. Mr. Quiet's house is surrounded by trees.

surround

## swallow

When you swallow, food goes down your throat and into your stomach.

A swallow is a small bird with pointed wings.

## swan

A swan is a large water bird with white or black feathers, a long, curved neck and webbed feet.

swan

sway

## sway

To sway is to move slowly from side to side. The branches of the trees swayed gently in the breeze.

## sweater

A sweater is a piece of knitted clothing worn on the top part of your body and on your arms.

## sweep

To sweep is to clean a floor using a brush or broom. In the fall, Mr. Fussy swept the leaves from his path several times a day.

## sweet

Sweet means not sour or salty. Sugar tastes sweet and so does food that has sugar in it, such as cake and candy.

## swell

To swell is to grow bigger or louder. When a river is higher after a heavy rain, we say that it is swollen.

O P Q R **S** T U V W X Y Z

### swim

To swim is to move through water using your arms and legs. Mr. Rush was swimming very fast. He swam across the lake in five minutes!

### swing

To swing is to move your body back and forth by hanging on to something with your arms. At the zoo, we watched as the monkeys swung on the bars in their cages.

A swing is a seat attached to an overhead frame or bar by chains or ropes.

### switch

A switch is a button or lever used to turn electricity on or off. You can switch a light on or off.

swing

### sword

A sword is a weapon with a long, sharp blade.

### symbol

A symbol is a mark that stands for something. The symbol = means "equals" and the symbol + means "add".

sword

### sympathy

When someone shows sympathy to you, he understands your problems and tries to help. Mr. Happy is a very sympathetic person. He listened to Mr. Miserable's problems and helped to cheer him up.

### syrup

Syrup is a thick, sweet liquid.

### system

A system is an orderly plan or a way to do things. Mr. Clever has a system to do everything.

## table

A table is a piece of furniture with a flat top and legs. You sit at a table to have your meals.

## tadpole

A tadpole is a young frog. Tadpoles live in the water and have tails that disappear as their legs and bodies grow.

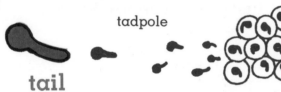

tadpole

## tail

The tail of an animal is the end part of its backbone. Dogs wag their tails when they are happy. Monkeys use their tails to swing from tree to tree.

tail

## take

When you take something you choose it. At the party, Mr. Greedy took the biggest piece of cake.

To take means to carry. Some children take their lunches to school.

To take also means to receive or accept, such as taking first prize.

To take also means to be doing something. You can take a dog for a walk or take a ride on a bus or take piano lessons.

To take can mean to make, as taking a picture.

take

To take can also mean to use up, as taking time to do something.

## tale

A tale is a story that can be true or untrue. The tale of Mr. Nonsense is about the silly things he does.

## talk

To talk means to speak and use words. Babies have to learn to talk. Mr. Chatterbox is always talking. He is talkative.

## tall

Tall means not short. Something that is tall goes high into the air Mr. Tall is very tall. So is a giraffe.

tall

## tame

A tame animal is one that is not wild. Cats and dogs are tame animals. If you tame an animal, you teach it to be friendly and to obey.

## tangle

To tangle is to twist things together so that they are difficult to take apart. Wool can get tangled while you are knitting.

## tank

A tank is a large container for holding liquids. A car has a gas tank.

## tap

A tap is a knob that you turn to allow liquid or gas to flow. A sink has hot and cold water taps.
   To tap means to knock something gently. You can make a tapping sound with your foot.

## tape

Tape is a long strip of material such as cloth or paper used to join things together.

## taste

When you taste something you put it in your mouth and find out what flavor it has. Sugar has a sweet taste. A lemon tastes sour.

## taxi

A taxi is a car that you pay the driver to ride in.

taxi

## tea

Tea is a drink made by pouring boiling water on dried leaves of the tea plant. You can put sugar and milk or lemon in tea.

### teach
To teach is to help a person to learn. Mr. Right taught Mr. Wrong how to do things properly.

### team
A team is a group of people who work or play together. A soccer team has eleven players.

telephone

team

### tear (It rhymes with bear.)
To tear is to pull apart. Mr. Grumpy cannot stand books. He tears the pages out instead of reading them. All of his books are torn.

### tear (It rhymes with hear.)
A tear is a drop of water that falls out of your eye when you cry.

### tease
To tease is to annoy someone in a playful way or to make fun of him or her. The clever elephant teased Mr. Dizzy by asking questions he couldn't answer.

### telephone
A telephone carries the sound of your voice. It allows you to speak with another person.

### television
Television sends and receives pictures and sounds. You can watch and listen to many different kinds of programs on television.

### tell
To tell someone something is to speak or write to him. Mr. Funny told Mr. Grumpy a joke to try to make him laugh.

To tell is also to count. Can you tell how many words are in this book?

### temper
Your temper is the way that you feel. When you become upset or angry, you lose your temper. Mr. Happy probably would not lose his temper.

### temperature
Temperature is a measure of how hot or cold something is. You use a thermometer to measure temperature.

## tempt

To tempt means to try and make someone do something. Mr. Greedy is often tempted to eat more than he should.

## tender

Tender means sore. If you bump your knee it will feel tender.

Tender also means kind and gentle.

Tender can also mean not tough. Tender meat is easy to cut and chew.

## tennis

Tennis is a game played with rackets. You hit a ball back and forth over a net.

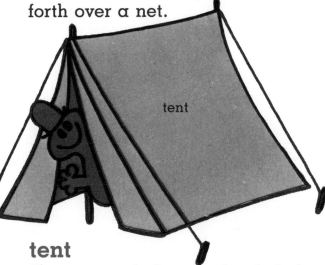

tent

## tent

A tent is a shelter made of cloth. It is held up by poles and tied with ropes to pegs in the ground.

## term

A term is a period of time with limits, as a term of office or a school term.

## terrible

Something terrible is very bad and often frightening. When you are sick, you feel terrible.

## terrified

If you are terrified you are very frightened. Most animals are terrified of fireworks.

## test

To test something is to try it out. Mr. Bounce tested his new heavy boots. He found that they stopped him from bouncing.

A test shows how well you can do something, such as a spelling test.

test

## than

Than shows how things or people are different. Mr. Tall is taller than all of his friends.

## thank

To thank someone is to say how pleased you are for something he or she has done for you.

## that

That refers to a person or thing. A cow is an animal that eats grass.

That can also refer to a particular person or thing. That is my coat.

## thaw

To thaw is to melt, to go from frozen to liquid. The ground is very wet when the snow thaws.

### the
The means one, usually one particular person or thing. Mr. Strong kicked the football over the house.

### theater
A theater is a special building where you can go to see plays or shows or movies.

### their
Their means belonging to more than one person. Jill and Mark live in a red house. Their house is red. The red house is theirs.

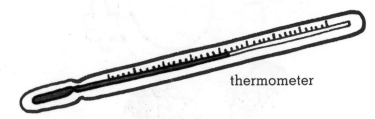

thermometer

### them
Them refers to more than one person or thing. When your hands are dirty, you wash them.

### then
Then means next or afterward. Mr. Lazy took a nap in his chair. Then he went to bed.

### there
There means in that place. Put the plate there.

There is used to call attention to something. There is snow on the roof.

### thermometer
A thermometer tells you how hot or cold someone or something is.

### they
They refers to more than one person or thing. I like books. They can help you learn. I read them often. Their pictures can be interesting.

### thick
Something that is thick is wide from side to side or from top to bottom. It is not thin.

### thief
A thief is a person who steals.

### thin
Thin means not fat or thick. Mr. Skinny is the thinnest of all the Mr. Men. No one is thinner.

### thing
A thing is an object or an action or a fact. You take your swimming things when you go to the beach. There are many things to do at the beach.

### think
When you think you use your mind. Mr. Bounce tried to think of a way to stop bouncing. Then he thought of a good idea. He went to see the doctor.

### thirsty
Thirsty means wanting or needing a drink. Hot weather can make you very thirsty.

### this
This means a particular thing. This book is a dictionary. These are my gloves. Those are your gloves.

## thorn
A thorn is a sharp point that grows on a plant.

## though
Though means although, or even if, or in spite of. Though it looks like rain, I am going to the ball game.

## thought
A thought is an idea or something you believe. The thought of a storm makes Mr. Nervous shake.

## thread
Thread is thin string. You sew with a needle and thread.

## threaten
To threaten is to say that you will do something unpleasant to someone. The wizard threatened to teach Mr. Mischief a lesson if he didn't stop playing tricks.

## throat
Your throat is inside your neck. You swallow food down your throat. Mr. Noisy got a sore throat from shouting.

## through
Through means from one side or from one end to the other. Mr. Nosey likes to look through people's windows.

Through also means by or in. You send a letter through the mail.

Through can mean finished. When he was through washing the dishes, Mr. Busy scrubbed the floor.

thunder

## throw
To throw means to make something go through the air with your hand. Mr. Strong threw a bowling ball across the park. Nobody had ever thrown one that far before.

## thumb
Your thumb is the shortest and thickest finger on your hand.

## thunder
Thunder is the loud noise that you hear during a storm. Mr. Nervous hides under the bed during a thunderstorm.

## tick
A tick is the sound made by a clock or watch.

A tick is also a small insect.

## ticket
A ticket is a piece of paper that you get when you pay to go on a plane, train or a bus or when you go to a play or a movie.

A ticket is also a piece of paper that tells how much something costs.

tie

## tickle

To tickle is to touch gently. This feeling makes you laugh. Mr. Tickle is always looking for someone to tickle.

## tidy

Tidy means neat and in order. Mr. Messy is not at all tidy.

## tie

To tie means to make a knot, usually with string or rope. Mr. Clumsy never ties his shoelaces.

A tie is a thin piece of material worn around the neck and tied with a knot. Ties are worn with shirts.

A tie is also an even score.

## tiger

A tiger is a fierce, wild animal that looks like a large cat. Tigers have orange fur with black stripes.

## tight

Tight means fitting close, not loose. Jane's shoes were so tight they hurt her feet.

## tights

Tights are clothing that are close fitting and worn on the feet, legs and lower part of the body.

## time

Time means the passing of minutes and hours and days. The time is a particular minute or hour or season, like Christmas time. You tell the time by reading the numbers on a clock.

To time something or someone is to measure the passing of time.

Time also means how often. When something is done again and again, it is done many times. Two times two is four.

## tiny

Tiny means very small. Mr. Small looks tiny beside Mr. Tall. Little Miss Tiny is even smaller.

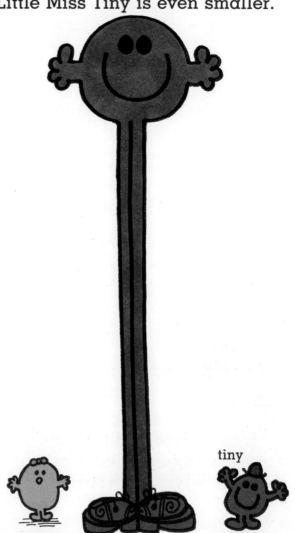

tiny

## tip

The tip is the ponited end of something, such as a pencil.

To tip means to upset or turn over. The chair tipped over when Mr. Bump walked into it.

A tip is money given to someone for doing something for you.

tiptoe

## tiptoe

To tiptoe means to walk on your toes. When you tiptoe you can move about very quietly.

## tire

A tire is the band of rubber or other material around the wheels of a car or bicycle.

To tire is to feel tired.

## tired

When you are tired you feel sleepy and want to rest. Mr. Lazy feels tired after walking to his front gate and back!

## title

A title is the name of something such as a book or a film or a song. The title of a book often tells you what it is about.

## to

To means for the purpose of. Mr. Silly and Mr. Nonsense used a rowboat to slide down the hill!

To means toward or in a direction. Throw the ball to me.

To can mean before or until or between. The time is five minutes to one. We will play ball from one o'clock to three o'clock.

To can also show how things compare, like the score of a game. Our team won, three to two.

## toast

Toast is bread that has been made brown and crisp by heat. Toast can be made in a toaster.

## today

Today means this day. If you finish your work today, you can play tomorrow.

## toe

A toe is a part of your foot. You have ten toes, five on each foot.

## together

Together means with each other. Mr. Bump and Mr. Strong went for a walk together.

together

229

### toilet

A toilet is found in the bathroom. It is used to carry away waste material by the use of water.

### tomato

A tomato is a round fruit that is usually eaten as a vegetable. Tomatoes have red skin and are soft and juicy inside.

tongue

### tomorrow

Tomorrow means the day after today.

### tongue

Your tongue is the part of your mouth that you use for licking and tasting. You also use your tongue when you are talking.

### tonight

Tonight means the night of this day.

### too

Too means more than enough. When Mr. Worry went for a walk he was worried that he might walk too far and be too tired to walk home.

Too also means as well as, or also. When Mr. Happy laughs, everyone else laughs, too.

tool

### tool

A tool is an instrument that helps us to do work. Carpenters use many different tools, such as hammers, nails and screwdrivers. A pencil is a writing tool.

### tooth

Each of the small white bones that grow out of your jaws is called a tooth. You use your teeth for biting and chewing.

### toothpaste

Toothpaste is used to clean your teeth. You squeeze it on to your toothbrush from a tube.

### top

The top is the highest part of something. Mr. Nonsense built his house at the top of a tree.

A top is a cover or lid. You take off the top of a bottle to use what is inside.

A top is also a toy that spins around and around.

topsy-turvy

## topsy-turvy

Topsy-turvy means confused, upside down, or back to front. Mr. Topsy-Turvy gets his words all mixed up when he talks. He also wears his hat upside down.

## tornado

A tornado is a violent wind storm.

## toss

To toss is to throw.

## total

Total means the whole. If you agree totally with someone, you agree with everything that person says or does.

A total is the whole amount. When you add numbers together the answer is called the total.

## touch

To touch something is to feel it. You put your hand on something lightly when you touch it. Mr. Robinson felt something touch his shoulder. It was Mr. Small.

## tough

Tough means very strong, or hard to break or tear. Some meat can be tough and hard to chew.

## tow

To tow is to pull or drag, as with a rope or chain.

## toward

If you move toward something, you move in the direction of it. Mr. Noisy is walking toward his house.

toward

## towel

A towel is a piece of cloth that is used to dry wet things. You dry yourself with a towel after you have a bath. Paper towels are sometimes used in the kitchen.

## tower

A tower is the upper, narrow part of a building or a tall, narrow building.

To tower is to rise above. Mr. Tall towers over everyone.

## town

A town is a collection of houses, stores and other buildings, and all the people living there. A town is smaller than a city.

town

tower

toys

## toy

A toy is something to play with. Dolls and model cars are toys. Mr. Snow helped Santa Claus deliver toys at Christmas.

## trace

To trace something means to copy or follow it exactly.

## track

A track is a set of marks left on the ground when a person, animal or vehicle has been over it. The tractor made a deep muddy track across the field.

A track is also the road or the rails on which a train runs.

## tractor

A tractor is a vehicle that is used to pull heavy loads.

tractor

## trade

Trade is buying and selling or changing one thing for another. Bob traded his baseball for John's football.

## traffic

Traffic means everything that moves by road, sea and air. When there is too much traffic at one time, there is a traffic jam, and nobody can move.

Traffic lights are a set of colored lights that tell drivers when to stop and when to go.

## train

A train is a vehicle that runs along a railroad track. Trains are made up of a number of cars pulled by an engine.

To train means to teach people or animals to do something. The boy trained his dog to sit up.

train

trample

## tramp
To tramp is to walk with a heavy step.

A tramp is a person who has no home and goes from city to city.

## trample
To trample means to step on and crush. A clumsy elephant walked into Mr. Fussy's garden and trampled his flowers!

## transport
To transport means to take people or things from one place to another. Buses and trains are kinds of transportation.

## trap
To trap is to catch and hold something or somebody. The miners were trapped underground by an explosion.

A trap is something for catching animals, such as a mouse trap.

## trash
Trash is anything that should be thrown away, not worth keeping.

tray

## travel
To travel means to go from one place to another. Mr. Rush is always traveling from one end of the country to the other, fast!

## tray
A tray is a flat piece of wood, tin or plastic that is used for carrying things. Trays are very useful.

## treasure
Treasure is a collection of valuable things. Divers search for hidden treasure in wrecked ships.

treasure

## treat
A treat is something that is very enjoyable and doesn't happen often. It is a treat to eat in a restaurant.

To treat means to behave towards someone in a certain way. If you treat your friends well, you are friendly and nice to them.

To treat also means to give medical attention. A doctor treats his or her patients and helps them to get well again. Sometimes they need special treatment.

233

tree

## tree

A tree is a large plant with a trunk, branches and leaves. Some trees lose their leaves in winter.

## tremble

To tremble means to shake from cold or fright. The slightest thing makes Mr. Nervous tremble. Even the sound of a leaf blowing makes him shake like jelly!

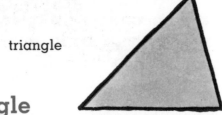

triangle

## triangle

A triangle is a shape with three sides and three points.

A triangle is also a musical instrument shaped like a triangle. It is made of metal and makes a ringing sound when you strike it.

## trick

A trick is an act to tease or annoy someone. Mr. Mischief is always playing tricks on people.

A trick is also a clever act done to amuse someone, as the tricks a magician does.

## trim

To trim is to make something neat by cutting it a bit shorter. Mr. Fussy has trimmed his moustache every day for years.

## trip

A trip is a journey or an outing or a short holiday. Jack went on a trip to Africa with Mr. Daydream.

To trip means to stumble or fall over something. Mr. Clumsy is always tripping over things. He even trips over his own feet!

## trouble

If you are in trouble, it means that you have done something wrong, or something unpleasant has happened to you. Little Miss Trouble caused a lot of trouble for Mr. Small. Then she was in trouble herself!

## trousers

Trousers are clothes that you wear on the lower part of your body. Trousers have separate parts to cover each leg.

trip

truck

## truck
A truck is a large vehicle used to carry heavy loads. Mr. Wrong got on a truck instead of a bus!

## true
If something is true it is correct and not false. It is not true to say that all birds can fly. It is true that all birds have beaks or bills.

## trumpet
A trumpet is a musical instrument made of brass, played

trumpet

by blowing through a mouthpiece.

## trunk
The trunk is the main part of a tree or a body. A tree trunk is covered with bark.

A trunk is a large, wooden or metal box with a lid for carrying clothes.

A trunk is also the long nose of an elephant.

## trust
To trust is to depend on someone to do something properly and honestly. The farmer trusts you to shut the gate when you leave the field.

## truth
The truth is something that is true. Mr. Stingy is not telling the truth when he tells people that he is poor. He has lots of money hidden away.

## try
To try means to do your best at something. In a race, everyone tries to win.

## tub
A tub is a large container for washing things in, such as a bathtub.

## tube
A tube is a long round pipe of metal, rubber or plastic.

## tulip
A tulip is a plant with a cup-shaped flower and long thin leaves. A tulip grows from a bulb.

## tumble
To tumble means to fall in a clumsy way. Mr. Bump tumbled down the steps.

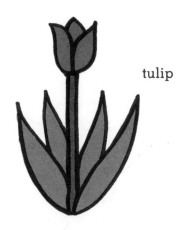

tulip

## tune

A tune is a series of notes that make a piece of music. You can play a tune on a piano.

## tunnel

A tunnel is a covered passage built under road, bridge or river, or through a hill or mountain.

## turkey

A turkey is a bird. Many people eat turkey for Thanksgiving and Christmas dinners.

## turn

A turn means a chance or a go. When you are playing a game you must wait for your turn.

turkey

To turn means to move around to face a different direction. The policeman turned around and saw Mr. Tickle.

To turn also means to change. The witch turned the prince into a frog.

## turtle

A turtle is a reptile that lives on land. A turtle has a hard shell on its back. It can pull its head and legs inside the shell.

## twice

Twice means two times.

twig

## twig

A twig is a very small branch of a tree or a bush. Some birds build their nests with twigs and grass.

## twin

Twins are two children who are born to the same mother at the same time. Twins sometimes look exactly alike, and it is hard to tell them apart.

## twist

To twist means to turn around and around. To open a bottle of soda you must twist the cap until it comes off.

## typewriter

A typewriter is a machine for writing letters and numbers. You type on a typewriter.

turn

## ugly

Ugly means unpleasant to look at, not beautiful. Monsters are ugly creatures.

## umbrella

You use an umbrella to keep you dry when it is raining. It has a handle and a piece of cloth stretched over a metal frame.

umbrella

## uncle

Your uncle is your mother's or father's brother or your aunt's husband.

## unconscious

When you are unconscious you lie still with your eyes closed, and you don't know what is going on around you. When you faint you are unconscious. A heavy blow on your head can also make you unconscious.

## under

Under means below or covered by. Mr. Small's house is under a daisy.

Under also means less than. You cannot drive a car if you are under age.

under

## understand

To understand something is to know what it means. Mr. Dizzy understood how to make tea after Mr. Clever explained it to him.

## uniform

A uniform means special clothes, all alike. Soldiers wear uniforms.

universe

## unite
To unite is to join together to become one. Fifty states are joined together to become one country, the United States of America.

## universe
The universe is all the planets and stars in space. Our world is only one very small part of the universe.

## unless
Unless means but not if. We will have a picnic unless it rains.

## until
Until means to a certain time. Mr. Stingy never buys a new pair of shoes until his old ones are full of holes.

## unusual
Unusual means strange or not common. It is very unusual for Mr. Slow to be on time.

## up
Up means away from the ground, the opposite of down. Mr. Bump started up the ladder.

Up also means to or toward a point, as in to pay up or to catch up.

uppity

## uppity
An uppity person thinks he is more important than everyone else. Mr. Uppity does not have many friends because he is so rude to everyone.

upset

useful

## use

To use means to do something with. You use money to buy things. We used all our money.

Useful means being of use or helpful. Mr.Clever has a very useful clock. It tells the time, says "Good morning," makes a cup of tea and shows the date and what the weather will be.

Useless means of no use at all.

## upset

To upset means to knock over. Mr. Clumsy upset a pile of cans in the supermarket.

Upset means unhappy. Claire was upset when she heard that her grandmother was not well.

## upstairs

Upstairs means one floor above. In many houses, the bedrooms are upstairs. You have to go up the stairs to get to them.

## urge

To urge means to try to make someone do something by talking him into it. After much urging, Mr. Miserable finally smiled.

## urgent

If something is urgent it is very important and needs attention right away. Mr. Rush is a good person to deliver an urgent message.

## usual

Usual means the way something or someone is most of the time. Mr. Happy is usually cheerful.

## utter

To utter means to speak. Mr. Quiet utters very few words.

## utterly

Utterly means completely. Mr. Silly was utterly amazed to see Mr. Impossible standing on no hands at the top of a lamp post!

## vacation

Vacation is the time away from such usual activities as work or school. Last year we spent our vacation at the beach.

valley

## valley

A valley is the low ground between two hills. A valley often has a stream or river running through it.

## value

The value of something is what makes it useful or desirable.

To value something is to think well of it and want to protect it. Something that has value is valuable.

## vanish

To vanish means to disappear suddenly. Mr. Impossible can make things vanish just by waving his hand.

## various

Various means several different kinds of. Mr. Quiet tried various jobs, but he wasn't very good at them. Finally, he got a job in a library.

## vase

A vase is a container for holding flowers. Vases can be many different shapes and sizes.

## vegetable

A vegetable is a plant that is grown for food. Cabbages, carrots, potatoes, cauliflowers and beans are all vegetables.

## vehicle

A vehicle is used to take people or goods from one place to another. Cars, trains and airplanes are all vehicles.

vehicles

## velvet

Velvet is a soft cloth. The threads stand up like short hairs.

## verse

A verse is a poem, or a line or part of a poem.

## very

Very means a large amount, more than usual. Mr. Tall is very tall.

## victory

Victory means winning a game or a battle. Our football team won a victory over the visiting team last Saturday.

## view

A view is what you can see from a certain place. Mr. Small has a nice view of the garden from his window.

## village

A village is a small town. It is all the buildings and all the people that are there.

## vine

A vine is a plant that grows very long, along the ground or upon something. Grapes and pumpkins grow on vines.

## violent

Violent means having great force or strength. A violent wind blew the roof off of the hen house.

## violin

A violin is a musical instrument that you play by touching the strings.

violent

## visit

To visit means to go to see or stay with someone. Mr. Skinny visited Mr. Greedy. Mr. Skinny was a visitor at Mr. Greedy's house.

## voice

Your voice is the sound that comes out of your mouth when you speak or sing.

## volunteer

To volunteer is to offer to do something without being asked. Mr. Happy volunteered to help the farmer feed his chickens.

## vote

To vote is to make a choice, choosing someone or something for a special purpose. You can vote for someone to be president of your club.

### wag
To wag is to move from side to side, as in a dog wagging its tail.

### wagon
A wagon is a vehicle with four wheels used to carry things.

### waist
Your waist is the narrow middle part of your body, between your chest and your hips.

### wait
To wait means to stay somewhere until something has happened or somebody has arrived. You wait for a bus at a bus stop.

### wake
To wake is to no longer be asleep or to make someone else no longer be asleep. When you wake up, you are awake. Mr. Noisy woke Mr. Lazy.

### walk
To walk means to move on foot. Mr. Tall can walk a very long way in a very short time with his long legs.

### wall
Walls are the sides of a building or a room.

A wall can also be a fence. Mr. Nosey likes looking around walls to see what is going on.

### wand
A wand is a stick used by a magician. It is supposed to help him do tricks.

### want
To want something is to wish for it. Mr. Greedy always wants the biggest piece of cake.

### war
A war is a battle between countries. Soldiers fight in wars.

### warm
Warm means fairly hot. Gloves keep your hands warm when the weather is cold.

### warn
To warn is to tell someone about danger that might happen. A fire alarm warns people when there is a fire.

wall

## was

Was means before now. It was raining, but now the sun is shining.

wash

## wash

To wash means to clean with water. Mrs. Washer washes clothes all day long.

## wasp

A wasp is a black and yellow insect that stings. A wasp makes a buzzing noise when it flies.

## waste

To waste means to use carelessly. Mr. Lazy wastes a lot of time sleeping.

Waste is something not able to be used or already used up. A waste paper basket is a place for paper and other trash.

## watch

To watch means to look at. Paul watched his father fix the car.

To watch also means to look after or take care of. Debbie watched the baby for her mother.

To watch also means to be careful. Watch where you are walking!

A watch is a small clock. Mr. Forgetful keeps forgetting to wind his watch, so he never knows what time it is.

## water

Water is a clear liquid. Water falls as rain and is found in rivers and lakes and seas.

## watermelon

A watermelon is a large green fruit with a soft inside that is pink or red.

## wave

A wave is a shape or movement that goes up and down. Jesse has waves in her hair. Her hair is wavy.

## wax

Wax is a hard substance that melts when it is hot. Candles and floor polish are made of wax.

## way

The way is a path or direction. An arrow shows the way to go.

The way is also how you do something. Mr. Topsy-Turvy does things in funny ways. He reads a book upside down!

way

## we

We and us are words you use when you talk about yourself together with other people. We, John and I, are walking to school. Will you walk with us?

## weak

Weak means not strong.

## weapon

A weapon is used for fighting or for hunting. Guns, swords and knives are weapons.

weave

## weave

To weave is to make threads into cloth. A machine called a loom is used for weaving. Mr. Busy wove a beautiful rug.

## web

A web is a fine net woven by a spider. Spiders catch flies in their webs.

A web is also the skin that grows between the toes of waterfowl, such as ducks and swans.

wear

## wear

To wear means to have clothes on. Mr. Nonsense wears a green hat and blue and white shoes.

To wear out means to use something so much that it is no longer any good. Mr. Busy wore out his shoes.

To wear out also means to make someone very tired. Mr. Lazy was worn out after a very short walk.

## weather

Weather is what it is like outside. The weather forecast tells you how hot or cold it will be, and if it is going to rain or snow.

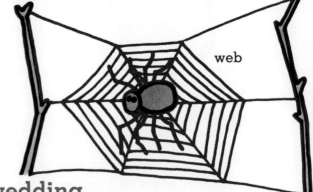

web

## wedding

A wedding is when a man and a woman get married.

## weed

A weed is a wild plant that grows where it is not wanted. Mr. Fussy pulls up all the weeds in his garden as soon as they appear.

| DAYS OF THE WEEK | |
|---|---|
| SUNDAY | |
| MONDAY | |
| TUESDAY | |
| WEDNESDAY | |
| THURSDAY | |
| FRIDAY | |
| SATURDAY | |

## week

week

A week is seven days. There are 52 weeks in a year. Saturday and Sunday are called the weekend.

## weep

To weep is to cry tears. Mary started to weep. She wept until she found her mother.

## weigh

To weigh means to find out how heavy something is. Mr. Greedy weighs a lot. He was not happy when he saw his weight on the scale.

weigh

## welcome

To welcome means to greet in a friendly way. Mr. Happy always welcomes his guests at the door.

When someone thanks you, you say, "You are welcome," which means, "That's all right, enjoy it."

## well

Well means in good health. When you are well, you feel good.

Well also means in a good way. Mr. Clever fixed his chair very well so it would not break again.

A well is a deep hole in the ground which may have water or oil at the bottom of it. People drill wells to search for water and oil.

## went

Went means has gone. Mr. Greedy went to the store.

## were

Were means before now. Where were you? I was waiting here.

## west

West is a direction. The sun sets in the west. California is in the western part of the United States.

## wet

Wet means soaked with a liquid and not dry. Mr. Grumpy's hat got wet in the rain.

## whale

A whale is the largest mammal found in the sea. It has a tail like a fish and spouts water through a hole at the top of its back.

whale

wheel

## what

What is used to ask questions of identification. What is that?

## wheel

A wheel is a round object that rolls. Wheels help vehicles to move along smoothly.

## when

When refers to time. Mr. Greedy eats when he is hungry. When did Mr. Bump fall?

## where

Where means the place something or someone is or was or will be. Mr. Forgetful never remembers where anything is.

## whether

Whether means if and shows alternatives. We are going to play tennis whether it rains or not.

## which

Which shows choices. Which color do you like best?

Which also means a thing already mentioned. Mr. Greedy ate the cake which he liked.

## while

While means a short time. Mr. Skinny stayed with Mr. Greedy for a while.

While also means at the same time. Mr. Clever read a book while Mr. Fussy cleaned.

## whisker

Whiskers are the stiff hairs that grow on men's faces and on some animals. A cat has long whiskers.

whistle

## whisper

To whisper means to speak very quietly. You whisper to someone if you don't want others to hear.

## whistle

To whistle is to make a high, thin sound by blowing through a small opening between your lips.

A whistle is a small object that makes a shrill note when it is blown.

## white

White is the color of snow. Mr. Slow has a white moustache.

## who

Who means what person. Who lives in that house? Whose house is it? To whom does the house belong?

## whole

Whole means complete. Mr. Small ate one whole bean for lunch today.

## why

Why means for what reason or purpose. Mr. Skinny doesn't know why he is never hungry.

## wicked

A wicked person is very bad. Mr. Clever read about a wicked witch who turned people into animals.

## wide

Wide means long from one side to the other. Mr. Uppity has a very wide gate so he can drive his enormous car through it.

## wife

A wife is a woman married to a man. The man she is married to is her husband.

## wild

Wild means living or growing naturally, not tame. Lions and tigers are wild animals. Dandelions are wild flowers.

a windy day

## will

Will means happening in the future, or expected to happen. Mr. Slow will always be late.

Will also means the ability to act or choose.

window

## win

To win is to be first or to do better than everyone else in a race or an election. Mr. Silly won the Nonsense Prize.

## wind

The wind is moving air. A strong wind blows people's hats off and can even blow down trees.

## wind (It rhymes with find.)

To wind means to turn something around and around, like winding a watch. Mr. Fussy wound his watch.

## window

A window is an opening in the wall of a building that lets in light and air. Windows usually have glass in them.

wink

## wing
A wing is the part of a bird's or an insect's body that is used for flying.

A wing is also the part of an airplane that sticks out on either side. The wings help to keep the plane in the air.

## wink
To wink is to shut one eye and open it again very quickly. Mr. Snow can wink his eye.

## winter
Winter is the coldest season of the year. Winter comes between autumn and spring.

## wipe
To wipe is to dry or clean something by rubbing it with a cloth. When you have washed the dishes, you wipe them with a towel to dry them.

## wire
Wire is a thin thread of metal that bends. Wires are used to carry electricity.

## wise
Wise means knowing a lot and behaving in a sensible way.

## wish
To wish for something is to want it very much and hope you can have it.

## witch
A witch is a woman who is supposed to make magic spells. You read about witches in stories.

## with
With means together or by the side of. Mr. Silly walked with Mr. Nonsense.

With also means using or having. Mr. Snow is the one with a scarf. All of his friends are without scarves.

witch

## within
Within means inside of or part of.

## wizard
A wizard is a man who is supposed to do magic. You read about wizards in fairy tales.

wobble

## wonderful
Wonderful means very good or amazing or beautiful. Mr. Tickle had a wonderful time in the park. He tickled everybody he could find!

## wobble
Something that wobbles is very shaky and moves from side to side. Bill couldn't balance on his bike. He wobbled from side to side and finally fell off!

wolf

## wolf
A wolf is a wild animal that looks like a large dog. Wolves make howling noises.

## woman
A woman is an adult female person. My mother and my grandmother are women.

## wonder
To wonder is to want to know more about something. Mr. Skinny wonders why he is never hungry.

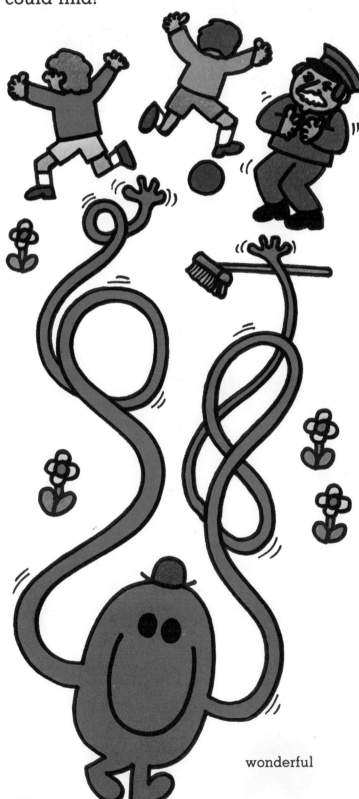

wonderful

woods

## wood

The trunks and branches of trees are wood. Wood is used for building many things such as houses and furniture.

Places where many trees grow close together are called woods or forests.

wool

## wool

Wool is the hair that grows on sheep. It is made into thread, and used for clothes and blankets.

## word

A word is a group of letters or sounds that together say something we can understand. Several words are used to make a sentence. There are thousands of words in this dictionary!

## work

To work is to do something that takes effort or energy. Mr. Busy works very hard every day. Jane turned the switch on to see if the light was working.

To work also means to have a job. Mr. Quiet works in a library.

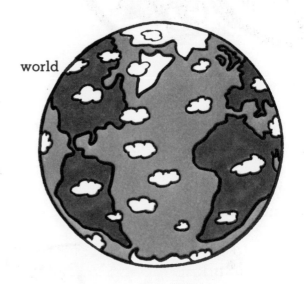

world

## world

The world is the earth and everything on it and in the sky above it. Mr. Daydream travels all over the world on his adventures.

## worm

A worm is a small creature that slides on the ground like a very small snake. Worms live in the soil.

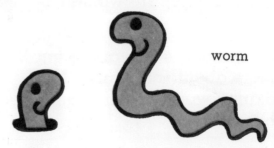

worm

## worry

To worry is to be anxious or bothered about something. Mr. Worry is always worried. He even worries about having nothing to worry about!

## worse

Worse means not as good as. Allan's voice is worse than Joe's. His mother's voice is the worst of all.

## worth

Worth means having value. When Mr. Clumsy broke his teapot, he decided that it wasn't worth mending. It was already full of cracks and chips.

## would

Would refers to the future. Would means might or will. Mr. Slow would be late for his own party!

## wrap

To wrap is to cover something all around with paper or cloth. Birthday presents are wrapped in pretty wrapping paper.

## wreck

To wreck is to destroy something or break it up completely. The ship was wrecked when it crashed into some rocks.

write

## wrist

Your wrist is the part of your body where your hand joins your arm.

## write

To write is to put down words on paper with a pen or pencil so that people can read them. Mr. Worry wrote a list of all the things he worries about. The written list was very long.

## wrong

Wrong means not right. Mr. Wrong never does anything right!

wreck

### x-ray

An x-ray machine is like a camera. It takes pictures through your skin of the insides of your body.

### xylophone

A xylophone is a musical instrument with wooden bars.

xylophone

### yard

A yard is the ground around a house. Mr. Messy's yard is always a mess.

A yard is also a measurement. A yard equals three feet.

### yawn

To yawn is to open your mouth very wide and take a deep breath. You yawn because you are tired or bored.

### year

A year is an amount of time that is 12 months or 52 weeks or 365 days. You have a birthday every year.

### yell

To yell is to call out in a very loud voice, as Mr. Noisy does.

### yellow

Yellow is the color of a banana.

### yes

When you say "Yes," it means you agree with someone or something.

### yesterday

Yesterday is the day before today.

yellow

### yet

Yet means up to this time or before this time. Have you had lunch yet?

Yet also means this soon. Don't eat your ice cream yet.

### yolk

A yolk is the yellow part of an egg.

### you

You is the word used to talk to another person. Mr. Clever asked Mr. Happy, "Can you lend me your pencil? I will give it back because it is yours."

## young

Young means not old. A lamb is a young sheep. David is younger than Andy. Andy is eight years old, and David is four years old. Both boys are youngsters.

## youth

Youth is the time of being young. A youth is a young person.

## zebra

A zebra is an animal that has dark and light stripes. Zebras look like small horses.

## zipper

A zipper is a metal or plastic fastener with a piece that moves up and down to open or close it. Zippers are used on jackets to keep them closed. You zip a zipper.

## zoo

A zoo is a place where wild animals are kept so that people can see them. Many of the animals are kept in cages. Mr. Funny and his friends went to the zoo.

zebra

zoo

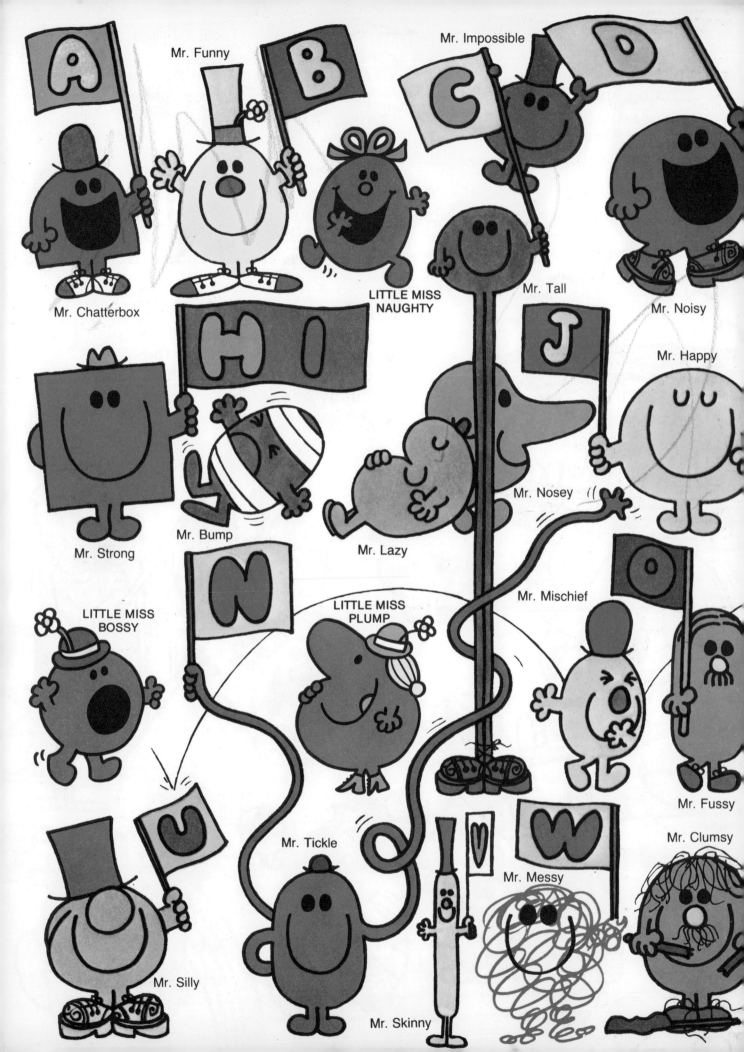